KATRIJN STEENBEKE &
ANN-SOPHIE DEPREZ

TEAM SMILE

creating a workplace where
everyone feels good

Lannoo
Campus

D/2024/45/499 – ISBN 978 90 209 2659 0 – NUR 800

Vormgeving omslag: Gert Degrande | De Witlofcompagnie
Vormgeving binnenwerk: Adept vormgeving

Uitgeverij LannooCampus
Vaartkom 41 bus 01.02
3000 Leuven
België

Postbus 23202
1100 DS Amsterdam
Nederland

www.lannoocampus.com

CONTENTS

Welcome 7

Positive psychology - How it all started 11
A definition 12
Optimal functioning of individuals, groups, and organisations ... 13

Culture 19
How does culture take shape? 20
Organisational culture 21

ENGAGEMENT - 'The engaged life' 25
A first habit: taking others along towards the future ... 26
A second habit: dynamizing with words, symbols and rituals ... 37
A third habit: generating engagement by recognising successes ... 46
A fourth habit: challenging the process with ideas ... 53

AMBIANCE - From 'ill-being' to 'well-being' 63
A first habit: energising people with positive interactions ... 64
A second habit: being grateful and expressing it ... 69
A third habit: contributing to a climate of trust ... 74
A fourth habit: creating opportunities for enjoyment ... 80

CONNECTION - Without connection no harmony ... 87
A first habit: seeing, hearing, and feeling qualities ... 88
A second habit: stimulating making the most of qualities ... 95
A third habit: connecting with the head and the heart ... 98
A fourth habit: supporting in positive and negative situations ... 107

MINDSET - Mindset 'hygiene' 115
A first habit: helping people feel valued 116
A second habit: seeing solutions rather than problems ... 121
A third habit: working in flow 128
A fourth habit: seeking feedback and feedforward ... 133

COMMUNICATION - You get what you give 141
A first habit: inspiring around the vision and objectives ... 142
A second habit: consciously using positive statements ... 147
A third habit: giving room for opinions and interaction ... 152
A fourth habit: conveying hope and optimism ... 158

Back to our desire 169
Acknowledgements 171
Sources 173

'If we are to preserve culture,
we must continue to create it.'

JOHAN HUIZINGA

WELCOME

We live in a turbulent era: economic crises, globalization, social and demographic shifts, pandemics, technological revolutions, and geopolitical crises. In these times, we must stay resilient. Well-being demands our attention. Transition, evolution, change, and revolution require courage and flexibility from everyone. Organisations are searching. Well-being is a growing need. It is a recurring demand in many of our projects across various sectors.

From our practice, we have seen and experienced the 'inner workings' of many organisations. We do not want to stand on the sidelines. Years ago, we sought a way to support organisations and discovered positive psychology. Positive psychology is a dynamic way to work towards the 'flourishing' of yourself, your team, and your organization, in any context. We were moved and inspired by it.

For many years, we have facilitated a wide range of development trajectories. Introducing positive psychology into organisations has had a positive impact on the culture within them. This was and remains our conviction. We had the opportunity to gain practical experiences in all possible market segments. We searched for patterns in organisations that either strengthened or hindered the culture. We researched which habits are necessary to move towards a positive organizational culture and experience well-being. After all, culture is the powerful, beating heart of every organization. People create that culture, and in turn, that culture shapes people.

We are different from others in this regard. "Yeah, right," you might be thinking now ⌣. And yet, it's true. There has been so much research and writing on talents, qualities, optimism, flow, mindset, self-leadership, workplace happiness, and so on. But what we couldn't find anywhere was a coherent and practical translation for organisations. That was the beginning of our journey. Reading, testing, writing, reworking, retesting, stepping back, diving back in, refining, and so forth. This is how corporate positivity® grew: the method to bring a fresh breeze through organisations.

Corporate positivity helps in recruitment by attracting talents. Loyalty also grows. Employees enjoy being with an employer where they feel good and look forward to going to work every day. A positive culture also facilitates social interaction, teamwork, and open communication. There is more fun, motivation, and energy in a positive environment. Finally, the link between strong corporate cultures and results is clear.

We are firmly convinced that corporate positivity makes a positive contribution. Focusing on corporate positivity contributes to well-being in an energetic culture. It is our mission to inspire people around this concept and to launch it into the world together with a team of corporate positivity activists. In this book, we address everyone working in human resources, every manager, C-level executives, and experts. But the book is, of course, aimed at anyone who wants to contribute to a positive corporate culture. Not tomorrow, but today.

Go in search of your smile, have a wonderful journey of discovery!

Positive
mindset
Positive
communication
Positive
engagement
Positive
ambiance
Positive
connection
CORPORATE
POSITIVITY®

POSITIVE PSYCHOLOGY
HOW IT ALL STARTED

It is 1997. Somewhere on a beach in Kona, a resort town on the west coast of Hawaii, two men meet seemingly by chance. Martin Seligman, an American psychologist and scientist, is at that time working on learned optimism. Mihaly Csikszentmihalyi, a Hungarian psychologist and researcher, is studying flow. On the beach in Kona, Csikszentmihalyi is taken by surprise by the power of the ocean. He unfortunately collides with a volcanic rock. Seligman witnesses the accident and helps him to a first aid station on the beach. The rest is history. The two men find common ground in a shared belief: traditional psychology is too heavily focused on addressing psychological issues such as trauma, anxiety, and depression.

Their days on the island are subsequently filled with discussions about what is missing in traditional psychology. They both believe that focusing on human strengths, qualities, and optimal functioning, rather than a focus on dysfunction, can lead to wonderful outcomes, to the 'flourishing of people'. They inspire one another with a shared passion to do something about it. They set to work as convinced activists in the field of positive psychology. By 1998, they manage to put positive psychology on the agenda at the annual conference of the American Psychology Association (APA). This proves to be a great success. Conferences worldwide quickly follow. Positive psychology is born.

Positive psychology has grown into a recognised movement within the science of psychology. It is not a different science in itself. It uses the same scientific research methods. What differs are the subjects of study and research and the questions being asked: 'What works?' rather than 'What doesn't work?'; 'In what areas does a person function well?' rather than 'What is the person's dysfunction?'. A renewed realism. No 'happyology', no magic wand, no toxic positivity. Positive psychology has three core ingredients: acknowledging what is not going well, reinforcing what is going well, and exploring where you want to go. In the meantime, positive psychology has become a field that fascinates numerous scientists. Among others, Barbara Frederickson, Ilona Boniwell, Scott Berry Kaufman, Corey Keyes, Christopher Peterson, and Martin Seligman continue to advance it to this day.

A DEFINITION

For a long time, traditional psychology focused on dysfunction. There is a historical explanation for this. Between the two World Wars, three goals were defined in the field of psychology: processing trauma; giving more meaning to life; and cultivating talents. After the Second World War, the latter two goals were largely lost. Psychological science began to concentrate on the first objective. It is not surprising that after a human crisis of such magnitude, the focus and associated funds flowed towards the treatment of trauma.

This fundamental idea of an exclusive 'disease model' is now outdated. Since 1948, the World Health Organization (WHO) has defined health as physical, social, and mental well-being, not merely the absence of 'disease' or 'disorder'. The field is still finding its way. As is often the case with definitions: the deeper you dig, the more you discover. This is certainly true when we examine positive psychology. Below you will find a number of definitions. We do not aim for completeness in listing these definitions.

'Positive psychology is nothing more than the scientific study of human strengths and virtues.'
Sheldon, M. & King, L.

'The study of conditions under which people thrive and the techniques that promote human well-being.'
Steerneman, P.

'Positive psychology is the scientific study of what goes right in life, from birth to death and at all stops in between. It is a newly christened approach within psychology that seriously investigates what makes life most worth living.'
Peterson, C.

'The scientific study of optimal human functioning with the aim of discovering and promoting factors that allow individuals and communities to thrive.'
Seligman, M.

Ten years of reading and working around this theme led us to the following definition to achieve practical results: Positive psychology is the science of optimal functioning for individuals, groups, and organisations: emotionally, psychologically, and socially, in any context.

We explain below what the three layers of this definition concretely mean.

OPTIMAL FUNCTIONING OF INDIVIDUALS, GROUPS, AND ORGANISATIONS

The goal of positive psychology is to enhance flourishing. The founder of the concept of 'flourishing' is Corey Keyes. It is during his quest for more knowledge and insight into well-being that he centralised the concept of 'flourishing'. According to him, flourishing is not just about being happy, in the sense of a euphoric end state. It is about continuously working on yourself, continually developing yourself, and undertaking actions to change situations. This requires effort and dedication. Everyone can flourish, based on their own choices. When you flourish, you function better; you feel good; you do good for yourself, for others, and for society.

Emotional, Psychological, and Social Well-Being

Flourishing consists of three components: emotional, psychological, and social. Emotional functioning involves experiencing positive feelings, such as joy, love, wonder, gratitude, and pride. Psychological functioning describes having positive thoughts, such as focusing on and trusting in one's strengths, and concentrating on enhancing qualities. Social functioning pertains to experiencing positive processes, such as thriving in relationships, groups, communities, in any context.

Positive psychology is one of the fastest-growing subdisciplines in psychology. It finds its applications in many domains: neuroscience, criminology, risk management, positive health, positive coaching, and organisational psychology. The science provides us with elements that support and undermine well-being, through the efforts of academics, literature, professional associations, activism, and public opinion. Positive psychology offers unique opportunities to address societal challenges. However, we would like to add a side note. Positive psychology is also criticised for primarily focusing on findings from Western or European contexts: Western, European, Industrialised, Rich, and Democratic (WEIRD) contexts.

How is your mental health? Answer the fourteen questions in Table 1 about the past month.

TABLE 1. TEST YOUR MENTAL HEALTH						
In the past month, how often did you feel that...	Never	Rarely	Some-times	Regu-larly	Often	(Al-most) always
1. you were happy						
2. you were interested in life						
3. you were satisfied						
4. you made an important contribution to society						
5. you were part of a community (social group, neighbour-hood, town)						
6. our society is becoming better for people						
7. people are fundamentally good						
8. you understand how our society works						
9. you liked most aspects of your personality						
10. you could handle your daily responsibilities well						
11. you had warm and trusting relationships with others						
12. you were challenged to grow or become a better person						
13. you confidently thought and expressed your own ideas and opinions						
14. your life had direction or meaning						

- Your answers to questions 1 - 3 reflect your emotional well-being, the experience of positive emotions.
- Your answers to questions 4 – 8 reflect your social well-being, the experience of positive interactions.
- Your answers to questions 9 - 14 reflect your psychological well-being, the presence of positive thoughts.
- All answers combined reflect your overall positive mental health.

Well-being and wellness are described as synonyms in dictionaries and online. However, positive psychology makes a significant distinction between the two (Bohlmeijer, 2013). Well-being encompasses more than wellness. In well-being, we find the three components previously described: emotions, thoughts, and social interactions. Wellness is the degree to which someone feels good in their own skin. Consequently, it may only relate to one of the three components. Good news: our overall well-being is determined by 50% by our genes; 10% by circumstances, and 40% by behaviour and skills (Bohlmeijer, 2013). This means we hold the keys to maintaining or enhancing our well-being.

We hope that you, too, will be convinced of the impact of positive psychology on yourself and others.

CULTURE

Culture is, in essence, what humans create. Opposite to this stands 'nature'. Nature is what has arisen spontaneously and without human intervention. We provide a brief, theoretical description of the concept of 'culture'. What is culture? Just a handshake? Or rather a hug? Two kisses? Or three? Or four? How do you greet the people around you? Have you ever received a nose rub? Chances are, you haven't. But if you ask an Inuit, they will consider it a common practice.

It's fun to watch the video 'Greetings around the World'. It shows a tangible experience of culture. Culture is everywhere. Populations are characterised by their culture. Families, teams, and organisations also have their own culture. Culture is about 'behaviour', the way we do things. Culture is about 'us', what we as a group of individuals collectively do and share: values, beliefs, rituals, stories, heroes, habits, rules, language, and so on. All around the world, people create order out of chaos. This is how culture grows. Culture is a shared reality, and it is not static. Culture develops, along with the people creating it. Thus, culture is the most important binding agent of groups, of organisations and their leaders. Culture is what you and I teach each other. It is learned behaviour.

Culture has a visible side, but also an invisible side. The visible side includes the rituals, the habits, the behaviours. Everything people do and say. The invisible side is what lies beneath the surface: values, beliefs, and the unwritten rules that stem from them. We connect with what we find important, thereby transcending individual interests. This allows one to identify with the DNA of culture.

HOW DOES CULTURE TAKE SHAPE?

Culture is neither good nor bad. It also never stands still. Every expression of culture has, at some point, been beneficial to the members of its group. These are responses formulated to meet needs: questions about existence and survival, as well as questions about cooperation and relationship building. How do we adapt as a group? How do we function and communicate together? Braun and Kramer (2015) describe several apparent dualities in our needs that can help us better understand this social process in which people in a group interact:

- **Need for routine and stability versus the need for new connections and diversity**: we warmly welcome a new team member, yet at the same time, we hope that this new person does not propose too many changes to our way of working.
- **Need for group formation versus the need to be seen as an individual**: we value the annual team-building event, yet we also want to stand on stage to present a personal contribution during that day.
- **Need for hierarchy versus the need for equality and connection**: we find it necessary for someone to set the guidelines, yet we do not want a leader who acts in an authoritarian manner.

Culture is dynamic. It is a continuous whirlpool of events. Over generations, there is a certain continuity. At the same time, its content is continually adjusted by new generations, each looking at the past from their own perspective. This is how new patterns emerge within a culture. This also applies within organisations. Consider hybrid working: a few years ago, working from home was unthinkable in many organisations, but now it is often the norm. Think of the concept of 'open plan' offices: about ten years ago, many offices were converted from individual offices to a single open space. In the meantime, there has already been another adjustment: instead of providing one hundred percent office space for employees, it is now often reduced to eighty percent.

ORGANISATIONAL CULTURE

When we talk about organisational culture, we often refer to 'strong' cultures, 'toxic' cultures, 'customer-oriented' cultures, 'people-oriented' cultures, and 'innovative' cultures. Organisational culture is the set of shared written and unwritten norms, values, and behavioural rules that influence employees' functioning. It is the way things are done within an organisation.

 We believe in the power and energy of a positive culture. As early as 2015, Harvard Business Review reported that positive work cultures are more productive (Seppälä & Kameron, 2015). A positive culture requires a structured approach, and corporate positivity is the ideal method for this. The strength of the method lies in its guidance on creating a positive work culture and detailing how to achieve this. We filtered the most relevant concepts for organisations from positive psychology, making the method unique. It integrates five patterns that have the greatest impact on driving an organisational culture: engagement, ambiance, connection, mindset, and communication. These patterns emerge when developing certain habits. Figure 1 provides an overview of the five patterns, each with four habits. You can learn, deepen, and internalise them.

The patterns of engagement, ambiance, connection, mindset, and communication are dynamic. There is no specific order. Start with what appeals to you the most to get you moving. Each pattern also includes cases based on our experience, marked with an ⌣ icon. We encourage you to test and try things here and there, which you will also recognise by the ❯❯ icon.

This book provides both theoretical perspectives and real-life cases along with practical tips. Here's a tip to get you started: take notes of the tips you'd like to put into action immediately. This will get you moving. Together with Team Smile, this method has also been incorporated into the 360° corporate positivity®-scan and the corporate positivity® e-learning platform. Together, they are an ideal foundation for organisations that deliberately choose to create an environment where everyone feels good.

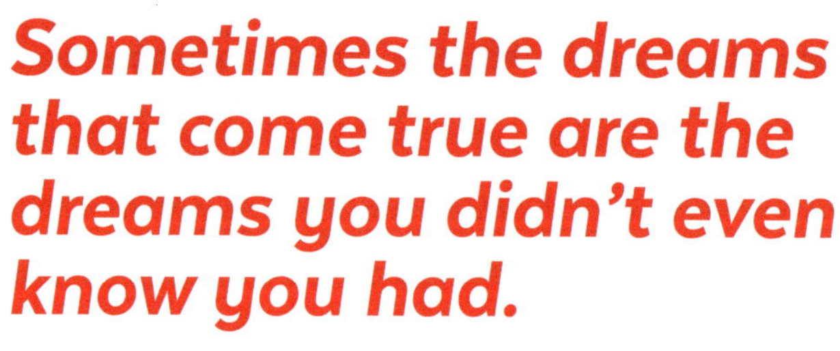

Positive engagement	Positive ambiance	Positive connections	Positive mindset	Positive communication
Takes others along towards the future	Energizes people with positive interactions	Sees, hears and feels qualities	Helps people feel valued	Inspires around the vision and objectives
Dynamizes with words, symbols and rituals	Is grateful and expresses it	Stimulates making the most of qualities	Sees solutions rather than problems	Consciously uses positive statements
Generates commitment by recognizing successes	Contributes to a climate of trust	Connects with the head and the heart	Works in flow	Gives room to opinions and interaction
Challenges the process with ideas	Creates opportunities for enjoyment	Supports in positive and negative situations	Seeks feedback and feedforward	Conveys hope and optimism

Figure 1. The five patterns and twenty habits of corporate positivity®

ENGAGEMENT

'THE ENGAGED LIFE'

Engagement, according to Martin Seligman, is a pillar of positive psychology in the concept of the engaged life (Seligman, Authentic Happiness, 2002). It is a life characterised by a combination of focus, concentration, interest, and enjoyment. This engagement can be directed towards oneself, others, the organisation, or society. Most research on this theme focuses on work. Positive engagement is an important predictor of an organisation's performance.

Facilitating engagement through positive psychology is a prerequisite for a dynamic culture.

Data analysis at our client reveals that the number of customers has declined by 26% over the past year. A decrease in revenue is a consequence. We are tasked with providing clarity through in-depth interviews. We question the entire management team. The new commercial strategy is at odds with past strategies. The team feels their past efforts are unrecognised. A pattern emerges. We observe resignation among the team members. Resignation also emerged in earlier decisions. This has an impact on engagement.

Positive engagement is a pattern of corporate positivity. If you want to move towards positive engagement with and within your organisation, the following four habits are recommended:
1. Taking others along towards the future
2. Dynamizing with words, symbols, and rituals
3. Generating engagement by recognising successes
4. Challenging the process with ideas

A FIRST HABIT: TAKING OTHERS ALONG TOWARDS THE FUTURE

It continues to surprise us that even today, change is still referred to with expressions such as 'dealing with change,' 'resistance to change,' 'change management,' 'managing change,' or 'the past was better.' It's high time to be awakened and to view change from a different perspective. We guide you through what you can do to embrace change: giving a voice to the minority, creating space for vulnerability, and bringing the organisation's values to life. By doing so, you take others along towards the future.

The way change is managed today has a significant impact on the culture of organisations. Providing insight into the need for change is usually the starting point for announcing it. Think of the impressive PowerPoint presentations where the entire organisation is scrutinised; mission, vision, values, and new plans are presented; the change is translated into projects and matrices, indeed, in Excel. This is where things start to go wrong. For us, it's a flashback to earlier times. We do not want to underestimate the complexity that change entails, but presenting change as a necessity rather than a desire generates negative emotions. As a result, we lose people along the way. They become rigid or cling to what is familiar. The impact is invisible but omnipresent.

Changes are cultural movements. They are entirely natural. All over the world, organisations change under the influence of external conditions or from the desire for growth and internal change. Positive thinking and feeling create a willingness to move. Essentially, we want to enable colleagues to take action. Building reliable relationships is the foundation for this. These relationships are the key to bringing others along into the new narrative. It is a process that begins when someone is willing to take risks and dares to be the first to open up, to show vulnerability, and to let go of control. Being the first to start requires courage, bravery, and a good dose of self-confidence. You are, after all, laying your cards on the table. You trust that others will take care of the information you communicate, the resources you allocate, and the feelings you share.

Embracing Change by Appealing to Reason and Emotion

One way to address both reason and emotion is by asking the right questions. Questions that are future-oriented drive us to take action. We leave the 'as is' behind and focus unconditionally on the 'to be'. We become engaged in the new narrative ‿ and become part of it. There are various questions we can ask ourselves in this process:

Questions from rational, logical, deductive, and numerical thinking:
- What qualities will help us achieve our goals?
- What strategic advantages will still be relevant tomorrow?
- What obstacles can we prepare for?
- What steps will we take?

Questions from emotion, intuition, creativity, and storytelling:
* What is the highest ambition we desire?
* What stories can we tell to inspire?
* What do we care about?
* How will we take care of each other?

Reason and emotion form a great duo. They are interconnected like yin and yang. They must be addressed in balance to respectfully bring others along in the movement.

The importance of the pattern of positive engagement can be read in the example from our practice below.

A new client comes knocking at our door with the following request: 'We are part of an international organisation, and many changes have occurred in recent years. Our local team is completely at loss. They feel isolated and we are concerned. Motivation levels have plummeted. Can you organise a "boost session" to get them enthusiastic again?' We choose a different approach. We conduct interviews with employees to uncover patterns within their team and the organisation. Our methodological findings reveal that the team culture is creating fields of suffocation and indifference. Engagement with the organisation is entirely missing. Our role is not to 'boost' but to create a positive movement together, allowing engagement to flourish once more.

We opt for systemic constellation, a method to map out the dynamics between team members. Underlying frustrations within the team, distrust in the strategy, and limiting beliefs surface. In the next step, team members visualise their desired future. Both we and management are pleasantly surprised by the outcome. We gain full team and leadership support for practical, small-scale commitments.

Engagement grows by affirming what remains, recognising and acknowledging it. Only then can employees let go of the past and build towards the future. It has taken many years to achieve what exists today. We should not assume that the work delivered has come about effortlessly. Therefore, pay attention not only to what changes but also to what already exists and will continue to exist. Communicate about both. Inspire and create enthusiasm.

'Ce qui est le plus dur pour un homme qui habiterait Vilvorde et qui veut aller à Hong Kong, ce n'est pas d'aller à Hong Kong mais de quitter Vilvorde.'

JACQUES BREL

The Power of the Minority

The minority perceives something that the rest have yet to see. Introducing movement into organisational culture is no longer about doing what the majority wants. It also involves listening to and being influenced by the vision of the minority. It is remarkable to dare to go against the current, just as a salmon does. It is remarkable to dare to stand up for your opinion in the midst of movement. It fosters ideas in others and opens eyes to things that are often overlooked.

Movement causes questions, reflections, and unrest. We consciously avoid talking about 'resistance' and instead refer to the voice of the minority. Resistance implies verbal and non-verbal opposition. Organisations label resistance as 'an issue' that needs to be addressed. We must admit. We used to have the same reaction. However, it is also valuable to give as much attention to the negative energy fields as to the positive energy that gradually emerges. Admit it, trying to move people by seducing and convincing them does not yield sustainable results.

We, corporate positivity activists, admire critical questions, considerations, and unrest. They provide a suitcase full of insights.

For us, it is essential to hear and observe the voice of the minority. It is a powerful force that enables a positive movement within a culture. Extensive research has been conducted in positive psychology on the functioning of organisations and communities. As humans, we are not isolated entities. We are fundamentally connected to other people. Co-existence is the fundamental characteristic of our lives. It is impossible to ignore the voice of the minority. In fact, it is a requirement to offer this voice a forum with a positive outlook, free from judgment and assumptions.

Would you also like to include the voice of the minority in the field of cultural movements? Here are some practical tips based on years of experience:

Don't:
- *Offer your solutions and ideas.*
- *Only organize formal moments.*
- *Centre explanations on the rational narrative.*
- *Promise miracles and a better world.*
- *Judge, despise, or criticise.*
- *Persuade and advise.*
- *Ask excessive and inappropriate questions.*
- *Deny and minimise.*
- *Hasten so that the voice of the minority does not get enough time and space.*

Do:
- *Allocate time and space so everyone can share their story formally and informally.*
- *Consider every thought or question as important.*
- *Look for the pattern within the unrest.*
- *Communicate about who (individual, team, organization) has taken which step, no matter how small it may seem.*
- *Ensure psychological safety.*
- *Actively seek out the critical voice.*
- *Organize group discussions.*
- *Communicate manoeuvring space transparently.*
- *Be willing to learn from each other.*
- *Believe that no one has a monopoly on the truth.*

Vulnerability on Stage

What do we mean by vulnerability? Being sensitive? Being emotional? A sign of weakness? When we introduce vulnerability to our clients, we notice there is a lot of confusion around the concept. Nowadays, we read a lot about vulnerability in the press, in trade journals, on LinkedIn. There is an uncomfortable connotation. We live in times where we are expected to be sharp and stand firmly.

Brené Brown, a professor of social work, has done extensive research on vulnerability. She writes: "Vulnerability sounds like truth and feels like courage. Truth and courage aren't always comfortable, but they're never weakness" (Brown, 2018). Being vulnerable means accepting uncertainty, exposing yourself emotionally, and daring to take risks. Vulnerability is the basis of emotions such as shame, fear, and disappointment. But it is also the birthplace of love, belonging, joy, empathy, innovation, and creativity. If we shut ourselves off from vulnerability, we close ourselves off from the experiences that give purpose and meaning to our lives.

When we decided to write our book and send our mission into the world, we were struck by our vulnerability. "Are we really authors?", "Can we say that?", "Do we have enough background?", "Will we inspire people?" It took us time and courage to share these emotions with each other and with others. "What if it goes wrong? How will we look?" It is precisely this vulnerability that has pushed us forward through trial and error. We took risks. We expressed emotions without shame. We built self-confidence step by step. And now we are incredibly proud of that ⌣.

Does it mean we put everything we think and feel on the table? That's not the point. We all have the right to set boundaries. It's okay to show vulnerability only when it's agreed upon with the other person. It's okay to share vulnerability only when you have completed your own processing.

Vulnerability in practice is putting yourself in a position where you can be rejected and, at the same time, where deep connection can arise. Vulnerability lies in actions and encourages action: telling a joke that might not be funny. Sitting at a table with people you don't know during a networking event. Expressing your feelings during a feedback conversation. In our development programmes, we teach our participants to harness the power of vulnerability for personal growth. Examining your thought patterns from a helicopter view helps with this.

- *Examine your thoughts:*
  - *What thoughts make it difficult for you to be vulnerable? What's wrong if people see that you don't do something 'right'? What's wrong if people see that you are not made of stone?*
- *Examine your fear:*
  - *What's the worst that could happen if you make yourself vulnerable?*
- *Accept the presence of fear:*
  - *You create peace of mind. You learn to put things into perspective and see new possibilities.*
- *Visualise your desire:*
  - *What do you really want? What would you love to do?*

Values on the Wall

Values should be reflected in practice, not just displayed on the wall. How often do we visit clients where beautiful brochures and frames are visible in the entrance hall and meeting rooms? These values are valuable. They make an organisation unique when they are embodied in everything the organisation stands for and does. It is truly possible to deeply integrate the values into the behaviour of everyone in the organisation. Here follows an impressive example of how this can be done. It fosters positive engagement.

**Without vulnerability
we do not exist**

**A person is not
available separately**

**I am in the group and
the group is in me**

**I am in the world and
the world is in me**

I am because we are

Several years ago, we were asked by an international organisation to train shop managers in leading their teams. The CEO had one condition for us: 'Take all the necessary time, even more than planned if needed, to convey our story and history to the participants. It doesn't matter how long they have been with us.' He further briefed us: 'When I speak to someone during a store visit, I always ask them to tell me our story. This is the soul of our organisation. If you don't know it, you cannot be truly engaged. We live our values in everything we do.' It was exceptional for us to have this expectation stated so explicitly. We translated this expectation into very concrete methodologies. Since our intervention, every 'milestone meeting' starts with a ritual. The shop managers can invite a colleague to step onto one of the company values displayed on a floor mat. The shop manager then explains what they have done specifically to bring this value to life within the team.

Values are often mentioned in the same breath as norms. However, they are something entirely different. Our norms are our rules of conduct, founded on our values. They are what we concretely do to express the values that are important to us. An example: respect is a value. Greeting everyone in the office cheerfully each morning is a behaviour, a translation of that value into a norm. This is self-evident for some, while others place more importance on always being punctual to translate that same value respect into a norm.

A new client contacts us to highlight the importance of corporate values among the leadership team. Upon further investigation, the real question is: 'How can we make our corporate values come alive in our organisation?' We translate the corporate values into concrete behaviours. From there, we delve into the competencies needed to make the value tangible. 'Tous ensemble' (All together) is a value in the organisation. We make it concrete by reflecting, both rationally and emotionally, on the questions 'What do you want to see, hear, and feel?' and 'What will ensure that everyone in the organisation experiences "Tous ensemble"?'

Can you name your organisation's values in one go? Tough question? And can you concretely describe the behaviour associated with these values? And one step further, do you know how to act upon this?

An example:
- *The value: 'pride is within me'*
- *The behaviour: I share success stories and achievements with colleagues*
- *A competency: focusing on positive language*

Values are important when taking others along towards the future since values are one of the cornerstones for fully experiencing the 'employee journey.' This journey starts from attracting talents: what perception do these talents have of the organisation? These new talents increasingly value the alignment between the organisation's values and their own. Can they connect their own being with the organisation's values? For human resources, this presents an incredible opportunity: in recruitment, we look at competencies, attitude, knowledge, and motivation. A question we ask ourselves: are the values not only mentioned but also made sufficiently tangible? Further along in the employee journey, the company values continue to have an impact: the integration at the start; the role of the manager; the opportunities for development; career advancement; collaboration; and so on.

Optimism, openness, and trust are our clear values.

A SECOND HABIT: DYNAMIZING WITH WORDS, SYMBOLS, AND RITUALS

Consciously working with rituals, symbols, and new words is quite new for many organisations. Yet they create a dynamic that is important in every organisation. It is absolutely fun to determine, together with employees, the rituals, words, and symbols that ensure dynamism, movement, and everyone's involvement. Some rituals are recurrent, others are one-off. Some symbols are particularly important, others less so. All these words, symbols, and rituals are the building blocks of the culture in which employees operate. We provide some examples and a link to a video later on to make it concrete.

Culture is largely learned. It is what is taught, shared, and passed down between people and generations. Because culture is something that can be 'learned', it is also something that can be 'adapted'. A perhaps universally recognisable translation of culture is the approach to time. We observe it with almost all our clients: dealing with time is part of the prevailing culture in the organisation. With one international client, time is strictly respected, even across borders. The way time is handled is part of the international culture. When a meeting starts at ten o'clock, everyone is in the room or logged in digitally by two minutes to ten at the latest. With another client, arriving or logging in five to even ten minutes late has become part of the culture. It is tolerated. It receives no attention. Everyone considers it 'normal'. In this chapter, we dissect what culture precisely is. After further clarifying the characteristics of culture, we guide you on how to use words, symbols, and rituals to make your organisational culture more dynamic.

Culture can be recognised by both observable and non-observable characteristics. Explicit behaviour is the most obvious expression of culture. It is observable and concerns the way people interact with each other, the language that is expected. Examples of explicit behaviour include decision-making, meeting culture, and leadership. Artefacts constitute the material culture and are the most open and observable expression of it: the buildings we work in, the decor of the lunchroom, the logos, the flags, and the clothes we wear. This is true in every environment. In a local business, it might be important to wear a tie for a business meeting, whereas, in the nearby IT company, sportswear on Friday might be part of the culture. It can also be the other way around.

Less directly observable are the norms. Norms are our habits in interactions. They make explicit how we want to interact with each other: rules of etiquette, politeness. Everyone likely considers it important to be polite and respectful, but what people specifically understand by politeness or respect can vary greatly. With some of our clients, we notice that it is an unspoken rule to place empty cups and glasses directly into the dishwasher. With other clients, this is not the case. Who in your organisation removes outdated information from the noticeboard? Every culture has numerous non-perceptible characteristics: implicit assumptions and values. It is what all members of the group consider correct and good. They lead to unspoken rules such as courage, fairness, kindness. The tie of the local entrepreneur is a good example of observable behaviour in our earlier description. The information on the noticeboard is an example of a non-perceptible assumption.

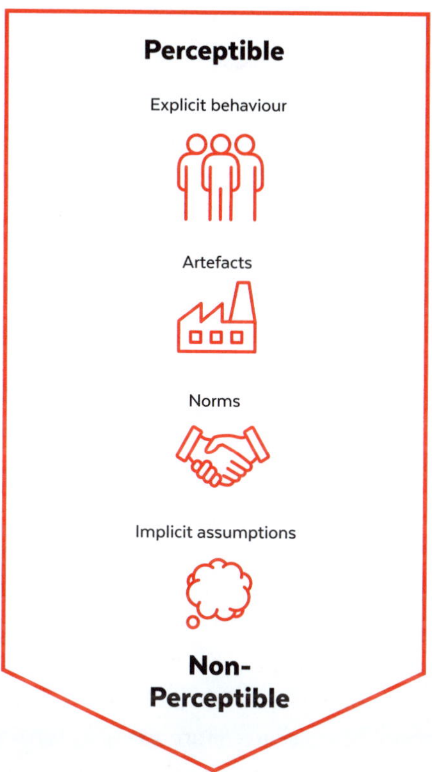

Figure 2. The different layers within a culture.

It is certainly worthwhile to consider the expressions of culture in your organisation as well. What are the characteristics of your organisation in these four layers: explicit behaviour; artefacts; norms; implicit assumptions? Do they ensure positive engagement? The unwritten rules, values, beliefs, and habits of an organisation unconsciously and unspokenly become a collective understanding: 'This is how we do things here.' As illustrated in the following case.

The Connecting and Energizing Power of Rituals

The desire to belong is ubiquitous. Herd animals, a colony of penguins, a pack of wolves, a school of dolphins. Humans also form groups. We often feel drawn to others who share the same values and beliefs as we do. Collaborating with like-minded individuals is comfortable, after all. We also mimic others for various reasons. When we conform to the group, there is less risk and uncertainty in the interaction. Sometimes we do this consciously. Often it is an unconscious process. This is how norms and habits develop in our interactions. For example: because almost everyone in the team goes to the pub on Friday, I go too. Emails are answered on the same working day, I strive to do the same.

As humans, we have the need to live in groups and involve others in that life. At the same time, we also want to be seen as individuals, separate from others. We have the need to establish hierarchy within groups. On the other hand, we long for equal treatment. Relationships form the core of our lives: at home, with our families, with our friends, at school, with colleagues at work, in groups and communities. The quality of these relationships determines our individual well-being and functioning, our sense of connection. There has been relatively little research on the optimal functioning of relationships. Positive psychology fills this gap. Martin Seligman identifies five components you can work on to experience well-being: positive emotions, engagement, relationships, meaning, and achievement. He takes a stand on this: 'Having positive relationships offers the best guarantee for experiencing the peaks of life. At the same time, they are the best antidote to the troughs of life.'

Rituals help in building those positive relationships. The power of rituals lies in the positive intention they carry. They foster connection and engagement. Rituals shape a culture. A ritual is a social action in which the values and identity of a group are displayed during a specific event. A ritual consists of several recognisable elements. It is repeated. It is planned. It has something special, apart from the everyday. Rituals often mark a transition to a new situation. They are then building blocks of the new culture.

Outside the work context, it is easy to think of examples where rituals connect and motivate. Think of a sports team that sings a specific song before playing a match. Do you know the famous 'Haka' in New Zealand? Were you baptised? Are you married? Do you give out presents at Christmas? These are all rituals.

Rituals also have a place at work, both in the team and at the organisational level. They bring connection. They are a must. They provide meaning and direction. They create a sense of group cohesion and build engagement. Rituals provide a sense of 'control' and therefore also safety. Rituals and their symbols help in celebrating, processing, connecting, or changing.

Here are some examples from workshops we facilitated: uncorking a bottle when a project is delivered; playing darts before starting focused work; beginning team meetings with personal music playlists; changing seats after a break in a meeting; whoever draws the lot is responsible for a treat for the next birthday in the team; when the same problem occurs more than three times, a 'fixathon' is planned; an 'energy buzzer' in the office when you want to receive a small boost from someone.

It is worthwhile to introduce new rituals. We use them to convey important messages, shape plans, and celebrate milestones. In this way, we provide meaning and context to events and to movement and change. Rituals have an impact. They help us distinguish between the extraordinary and the ordinary. They mark transitions and allow us to celebrate successes. There is a growing demand within organisations to collaboratively develop a concrete action plan around this.

How Do You Create Positive Rituals, Symbols, and Words?

To influence the culture of organisations and introduce positive rituals, we, as corporate positivity-activists, engage with the 'creators' of that culture. We delve into the organisation, the team, to discover what the current rituals and habits are; and to determine how we can introduce new positive rituals, symbols, and words in the future. With a clear view on the functioning of organisations from years of experience, we enhance positive engagement through new ideas, surprising rituals, unknown symbols, new routines, and so on. We are pleased to share a creative example of a ritual that stimulates the involvement of everyone in the organisation.

Carnival is a well-known celebration with a familiar ritual. By handing over the key, the mayor symbolically transfers his duties to the princes, who then govern the city for the four days of Carnival. Peer Swinkels, CEO of Royal Swinkels Family Brewer, a brewer of various famous European beers, incorporates this ritual into his company. During Carnival, he hands over the company's 'beer key' to the Carnival board. The business suit is swapped for a Carnival outfit. The period is clearly defined. Humorous feedback can be given to Mr Swinkels and is encouraged. A few days without deadlines, milestones, and top priorities. After the festivities, everyone returns to the proverbial business suit. Swinkels testifies that this annual company ritual fosters engagement, understanding, connection, and creativity.

We contacted Peer Swinkels to check if this ritual is still alive. He confirmed that it is. However, the business suit is not entirely accurate. Peer notes that casual attire is more fitting with the company's culture. Thank you for your pleasant responses, Peer!

Introducing positive rituals to increase engagement is a compelling exercise for any organisation.

Research into organisational rituals indicates that there are five domains where they can have a strong impact:

- Change and transition: managing unrest and the new.
- Creativity and innovation: generating better ideas and a stronger vision.
- Conflict and resilience: translating tensions into balance.
- Performance and flow: focus, confidence, and productivity.
- Group feeling: creating connection.

What comes to mind when you think about the rituals in your organisation? Can you list them easily? Are they energising and connecting rituals? Or is the dynamic missing? An assessment of the existing rituals and their impact is a good starting point.

If you want to discover an original example of a ritual, be sure to read the case below.

Here you can watch New Belgium's video about their rituals.

In our own professional activities, we notice that organisations, driven by great enthusiasm, tend to act ad hoc. However, we advise considering how rituals can find grounding within a narrative. This can be done in various ways. The employee journey is a good example. We will use this journey as an example underneath. Ensure you have answers to the following questions before delving into the rituals of the journey.

- What is the purpose of the ritual? Is it about connection, change, self-confidence, resilience, recognition?
- What are the different steps in the employee journey that the organization wishes to embed in rituals? Think of recruitment, successful completion of initial training, years of service, promotions, job rotations, successful project deliveries, initiation of coaching projects.
- Who are the participants in the ritual? The involved employee and their team? Other teams as well? External parties? Clients?
- Where does the ritual take place? Indoors? Outdoors? Digitally?
- Who is the facilitator of the ritual? Can we involve the executive team and senior management? Which department? Which employees? Or is it rather an external expert?

Rituals and symbols are a forgotten language. They are often considered too esoteric. Yet, people are ritualistic beings. Organisations focus heavily on thinking and doing: business results, production, P&L, marketing, and so on. Rituals, symbols, and words support the human side of the organization. They pay attention to the emotional world of employees, providing a different gateway to emotions. This, in turn, creates engagement.

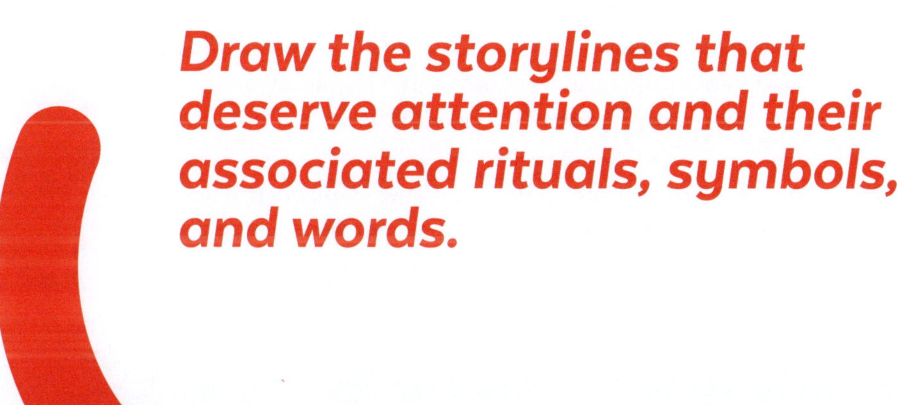

Draw the storylines that deserve attention and their associated rituals, symbols, and words.

A THIRD HABIT: GENERATING ENGAGEMENT BY RECOGNISING SUCCESSES

Motivation, Engagement, Commitment, Perseverance

We all prefer to associate with winners rather than losers. Don't you agree? When we see success being achieved, we are more committed. In his study, psychologist Karl Weick (2002) argues that the power of small wins is crucial in maintaining high motivation. Regularly achieving victories helps build and sustain positive long-term engagement. From a behavioural perspective, we tend to regard effort and perseverance as 'normal.' The small successes along the way are insufficiently acknowledged and celebrated. Naturally, we focus on what can be improved. However, from our experience, we observe a growing expectation among employees to give more attention to successes. In this chapter, we will tell you more about the lead-up to success; the four levels of motivation; the importance of attention; and the characteristics of the learning organisation. Only when successes are achieved can we recognise them and engagement grow.

To exert effort, motivation is necessary. What words best capture the essence of motivation? It is what moves you into action. What are the telltale indicators of motivation? A clear explanation of the four levels of motivation is provided by Deci and Ryan (1985). You can find them in figure 3.

- Intrinsic or integrated motivation aligns completely with our values and sense of purpose. For instance, you might volunteer to be a mentor for a new team member because you believe it is important for everyone to have fair opportunities for success.

- Identified motivation involves doing something because you understand its significance. For example, you are motivated to participate in a brainstorming session because your expertise adds value.

- Introjected motivation is doing something to avoid negative feelings such as fear, guilt, or shame. For instance, you attend a meeting that you don't see the point of because you fear the consequences of not participating.

- External motivation means being driven because something is required. For example, you must complete a report by a deadline, so you do it.

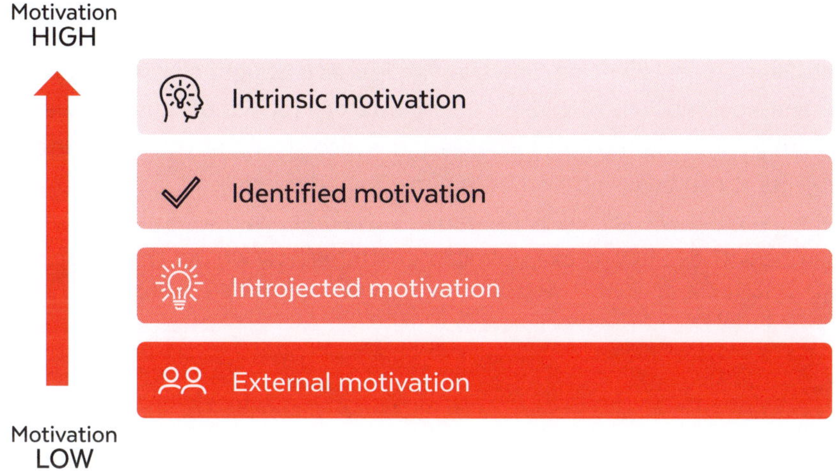

Figure 3. Motivation at Four Levels.

The more intrinsic or integrated motivation you experience, the higher your positive engagement. Engagement grows, generates commitment, and fosters perseverance. It is a positive process that is visible to yourself and others. However, this process does not come on a silver platter. How deeply does your motivation run? And that of your team members? It requires perseverance: continuing to work on something even when there are obstacles; repeating viewpoints and making suggestions; not being deterred by criticism or opposition to your ideas; knowing when to stop.

Visualisation is a powerful technique for perseverance and achieving goals. Suppose you need to give a presentation for work in front of a group of people. This makes many people nervous. What images do you conjure up for yourself? Do you see yourself turning 'red' in front of the group, or struggling with connecting the projector? Such images have a negative impact on your behaviour. From this state of mind, you take very different actions and achieve different results compared to when you visualise positive or neutral images in response to being asked to give a presentation. For example, think of the notes in your hand or the presence of your friendly IT colleague in the audience.

Research shows that visualising your path, actions, or steps to be taken more often turns a dream into reality. In business, visuals often play a secondary role. First, a text is written, and then an image is sought to accompany it. When visualisation is employed during strategy formation, it is a powerful tool to get people moving. Visualisation is also strong at the beginning of projects. It can be applied on both a macro and micro level. It can connect personal goals with those of the project, the organisation, and other team members. The following example demonstrates how we put this into practice as well.

If you can visualise it, you can actualise it.

Attention Leads to Flourishing

Aristotle's saying 'Everything you give attention to grows' is still relevant to-day. It is one of the key lessons from behavioural sciences. Receiving attention is a very fundamental and innate need in humans. Attachment to others provides certainty, safety, and protection. When you receive attention, you feel that you matter, are taken seriously, and are heard. Humans are social beings and need attention. We seek attention for who we are and what we do in all sorts of conscious and unconscious ways.

Turning our attention inward is the first step toward true flourishing, before we can hope for attention from others. Do you want to become proficient at using new software? Then use it more often. Do you enjoy being surrounded by new colleagues? Find opportunities to connect with them. Do you want to improve in project management? Express your desire to manage a project. Focusing attention on yourself is perfectly fine. It's a reciprocal process: you achieve success, it gets noticed, and you receive attention from others. The comparison with water is quite fitting. Just like water, attention costs virtually nothing. Water also fosters growth. In fact, without water, there is no life. Water sets things in motion, just as attention does. Giving attention to self and others lies in the small things. The case below exemplifies this.

Everything you give attention to grows.

Everything you share with others grows even more.

Success becomes a reality.

A Learning Organisation for Growth Opportunities and Success

A learning organisation is an entity that deliberately focuses on the qualitative and quantitative learning potential of its employees, teams, and the organisation as a whole. Learning organisations are agile, innovate faster, and foster greater team cohesion. They are attractive employers who motivate employees to develop in ways that are beneficial both to themselves and to the organisation. They implement a context where performance is facilitated and encouraged. Successes, including the small ones along the way, are acknowledged.

'The Fifth Discipline: The Art and Practice of the Learning Organisation'

One of the seminal works in the field of learning organisations is Peter Senge's book, The Fifth Discipline: The Art and Practice of the Learning Organisation. In his book, Senge outlines how a learning organisation can rapidly respond to changes by encouraging development and initiative. According to Senge, learning organisations operate based on five disciplines (see figure 4):

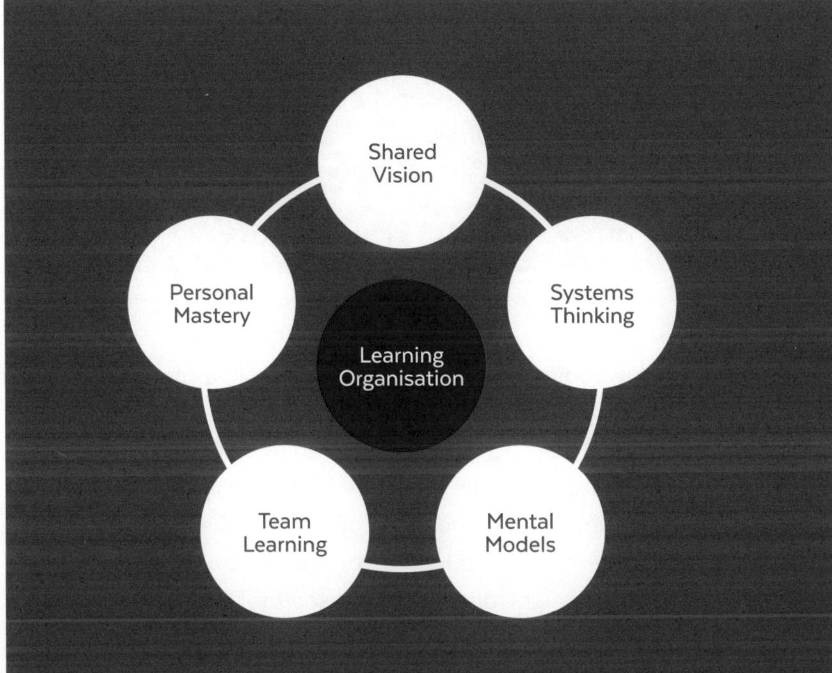

Figure 4. Senge's Five Disciplines.

Personal Mastery

Are you critical? Are you aware of your areas for development? The learning organisation is defined by the learning ability of its employees.

Mental Models

Is my truth your truth? In the learning organisation, there is a search for reinforcing and limiting beliefs.

Shared Vision

What is our future? The learning organisation envisions a promising future for its employees that they recognise and are eager to contribute to.

Team Learning

Learning alone or together? A learning organisation offers both individual and team learning.

As an employer, developing a learning organisation is a means to create engagement and recognise successes. Certificates, testimonials, incentives, badges, coins, applications, and so on have been used for years to provide recognition, and it continues to be effective. Does your organisation have a reputation among employees and in the market for being a learning organisation? Is learning recognised? In reality, we discover that fostering a learning culture is less straightforward than it seems. Learning is not a moment but a continuous process that requires ongoing attention. Throughout our careers, we have always worked in organisations where learning receives attention. Our expertise is sought to develop a motivating learning strategy.

'The magic is in the doing.'

A FOURTH HABIT: CHALLENGING THE PROCESS WITH IDEAS

What does this fourth habit entail? Here, you will learn about the power of understanding your life story to know your ambitions; how curiosity can help shape your future and thus challenge processes. Knowing your ambitions is the first step to setting us into motion. Getting into action starts with self-leadership. Self-awareness is the starting point of self-leadership. You know your qualities, strengths, and points of attention, your triggers, motivators, and goals. This strengthens self-confidence. From that self-confidence, you dare to question things. With that ambitious attitude, you excel at generating ideas and exploring possibilities.

Our knowledge and insight about what we want to contribute start with our own life story. Mapping out your own life story is a methodology that often forms the basis of the processes we facilitate with our clients. It gives us a very sharp and clear view of the power of self-knowledge and self-awareness. It's worthwhile to pause, take a blank sheet, and outline our personal history, with its highs and lows. That story makes us who we are. It shapes us. It is our view of the world. Can we also make connections between our history to date and what we want to contribute in the future? Do we understand who we are today and know who we want to be tomorrow? The following questions can help with this:

- What crossed your path?
- Who played an important role in your life?
- What has shaped you? What were the turning points in your life?
- What are important values for you?
- What patterns do you recognise in your life story?
- What do you learn from these patterns?
- How have you dealt with successes and setbacks?
- Which qualities have helped you in this?

The case below highlights the importance of reflecting on your life story to guide who you wish to become tomorrow.

We are facilitating a development programme on 'Positive Leadership' for our client. The first module in the programme is about mapping your inner compass. Self-knowledge is the starting point in understanding who you are and growing towards who you want to be. The participants work on an exercise about their peak moments and the lows in their life. Antonia shares her story with the group.

As a young girl, Antonia was overlooked by her father. He had hoped for a son, not a daughter. During her childhood, Antonia was systematically ignored by her father. Reflecting on this chapter, she recognises it as one of her life's lowest points. Today, in her role as an inclusion expert, she channels that experience with remarkable intensity. She now realises that this is an expression of her desire to be seen. This need stems from her life story. Her quality of independence helped her at the time. She recognises that while this is valuable, she tends to overuse this quality. She will try to better connect with kindness towards herself in the future. In doing so, she will learn to moderate her urge for independence.

Self-awareness brings us to our authentic core. It is an important step in discovering meaning. An important step in being who we want to be. Within the concept of meaning, there are different layers. Extrinsic meaning revolves around what we want, apart from ourselves: working to earn money, pursuing a promotion out of a desire for respect and authority, a nicer office or a bigger car for the sake of our image. Intrinsic meaning is about our own journey, what we personally find important: becoming an expert out of pure passion, acquiring a skill out of a desire for personal growth, leading a project because we strongly believe in it. We find something meaningful because it fosters our personal growth. We contribute to something larger than ourselves, the company vision, the 'bigger picture'. This holds a fundamental message for every organisation.

Time for a bold surge of activism.

Look back to move forward.

We have seen the inner workings of numerous organisations. Too often, we encounter confusion and 'quiet quitting', where employees limit their work to the bare minimum, unsure of 'why they are doing it' or unable to support it. 'Quiet quitters' often form a group that makes less noise. However, if there is no investment in the working relationship with these employees, it can undermine the company's culture. These individuals may eventually drop out, leave, or be left behind. Human resources and managers play a crucial role here. Do we have a clear understanding of what binds employees to our company? Can we distinguish between intrinsic and extrinsic meaning through an analytical lens? Who is just doing their job, and who is following their calling within the organisation?

Are you familiar with 'ikigai'?

Blue Zones are the places in the world where people live the longest. You can find them in Sardinia (Italy), Loma Linda (California), Nicoya (Costa Rica), Ikaria (Greece), and Okinawa (Japan). Research into the reasons for longevity in these zones reveals a few key factors: healthy eating; sufficient physical activity; having a social network; and having a purpose in life.

The island of Okinawa in Japan ranks number one on the list of Blue Zones. Researchers emphasise that the island's long lifespan is largely attributed to their 'ikigai mindset'. This grants their days a profound sense of meaning. According to Japanese tradition, ikigai is seen as something

Daring to Innovate

Many brilliant ideas are often viewed with suspicion at first. And yet, being engaged means daring to come forward with what you think, with your ideas and wild thoughts, in all your vulnerability. To thrive, organisations must go beyond business as usual. Everyone has a responsibility to dare to challenge the norm and embrace change. Questioning 'onboarding' processes; abolishing evaluations and replacing them with growth conversations; challenging the usefulness of 'open landscape' offices; abolishing mandatory training; assigning tasks based on interests and strengths; and so on. Another example is the case below with Greg Linden. It shows that everyone in the organisation can be a driving force for innovation and process improvement, across functions and domains. Giving everyone the chance to take initiative is a must and can bring about surprisingly positive changes.

Greg Linden, a recently hired employee at Amazon in 1997, came up with the idea of building an e-commerce recommendation engine: 'Customers who bought this also bought' or 'Suggestions for you.' He wondered if Amazon could encourage its customers to make the same kind of impulse purchases that supermarkets promote by placing sweets and other small items near the checkouts.

His colleagues were enthusiastic, but an influential vice president vetoed the idea. It would make the online checkout process too complex.

Greg Linden persisted, and a trial was set up. Today, 35% of Amazon's revenue is generated through such recommendations.

Mihaly Csikszentmihalyi, a positive psychologist, describes how creativity and innovation emerge. According to him, creativity does not occur within the minds of individuals. It takes place in the interaction between people's thoughts and their socio-cultural context. Creativity is a systemic phenomenon, not an individual one. It requires connection and engagement (Csikszentmihalyi, 2021).

Conformity or Curiosity?

Earlier, we discussed our herd mentality and how comfortable it can be to conform to the group. Conformist behaviour makes us cling to proven patterns from the past. Both large systems, such as societies and companies, and small systems, such as teams and individuals, constantly strive for a state of conformity. This gives us a sense of certainty and stability. To challenge the process with creative ideas and dare to think outside the box, psychological safety is indispensable. Being able to show and share your vulnerabilities is a prerequisite. Additionally, our mindset also plays an important role.

Stefaan Van Hooydonk is the founder of the Global Curiosity Institute and an advisor on fostering curiosity in the workplace. He advocates for curiosity over conformity. Curiosity challenges the status quo and the desire to prefer a comfortable past over an uncertain future. He translates curiosity into three applications.

- Intellectual curiosity: our curiosity about the world.
- Empathetic curiosity: our curiosity about others.
- Intrapersonal curiosity: our curiosity about ourselves.

Intellectual curiosity is the drive we have to know what is happening in the world. It translates into taking pleasure in learning something new, embracing change, and seeking more knowledge about the world. Einstein said of himself: 'I have no special talent. I am only passionately curious.'

Empathetic curiosity is about how open we are to others, their ideas, and their feelings. It translates into the extent to which we are interested in what others think and feel. It reflects how open we are to the ideas, emotions, and reactions of others. It teaches us how empathetic we are and how we can empathise with the perspectives of others. 'I don't really like that person. I want to get to know him better for that reason' is a good example of empathetic curiosity.

We just talked about understanding our own life history. That is intrapersonal curiosity. The more we know about ourselves, the more we can handle; the better we can view ourselves from a helicopter perspective and examine our own thoughts, feelings, and behaviour. We become a better version of ourselves. In the case below, you can discover the three forms of curiosity.

To truly challenge the process, we must let our curiosity lead us into the unknown. This can be done extensively through an online test provided by the Global Curiosity Institute. You can access and complete it directly via the link in the QR code. There, you will find 54 statements to score yourself on. You will receive your individual 'curiosity profile'. In preparation for workshops and coaching programmes, this gives both us and the participants insights into everyone's 'curiosity muscle'.

 The 54 statements from the online test reflect translations of the three domains of curiosity. We provide some examples.

Curiosity about the world

- I find it fascinating to learn new information.
- Risk-taking is exciting to me.
- I enjoy learning about subjects that are unfamiliar to me.
- I seek out situations where it is likely that I will have to think in depth about something.

Curiosity about others

- I try to understand people's feelings.
- I ask a lot of questions to find out what interests other people.
- When people quarrel, I like to know what is going on.
- When talking to someone who is excited, I am curious to find out why.

Curiosity about ourselves

- It is important to me to understand what my feelings mean.
- I really spend time in self-reflection.
- I usually have a very clear idea of why I have behaved in a certain way.
- I have a definite need to understand the way that my mind works.

According to LinkedIn data, in 2022, the use of the word 'curiosity' in job vacancies increased by 90% compared to 2021.

If you do ordinary things with absolute commitment, you become extraordinary.

Curious organisations challenge their processes

Starbucks Frappuccino entered the market after a district manager, Dina Campion, became frustrated that her customers were going to competing shops for cold blended drinks. At that time, Starbucks did not offer these. Dina had an idea. She was eager to experiment with recipes herself. Initially, she found no one to support her. Despite the odds, she persuaded a colleague to advocate for her. He bought her a blender. Dina took the initiative and started mixing cold drinks in one of her stores. She served her own concoctions to her customers and sought feedback. Gradually, the Starbucks management came to see its value and embraced the decision to invest; as more and more people began asking for her drinks. Starbucks launched the Frappuccino. It became the most successful launch in the company's history.

The role of human resources in the creative process of organisations is significant. We often quickly attribute this to departments like marketing and R&D. Understandably so. However, much creativity also lies in consciously listening to what others think and say when they put themselves in your shoes. It provides different perspectives. In our own professional activities, we have found that focusing on job rotation, working with roles rather than departments, recruiting based on qualities rather than degrees, and allowing time and space for personal projects, opens doors to the flow of creativity. As mentioned earlier, creativity is systemic. Psychological studies have proven that the engagement of everyone contributes to a positive organisational culture. Daniel Kahn (1990), for example, refers to engagement as 'the extent to which employees bring their personal identity to their work'. From who you are, you can lead others into the future; you dare to name and illustrate rituals and symbols; you acknowledge successes and dare to challenge existing processes with new ideas.

AMBIANCE

FROM 'ILL-BEING' TO 'WELL-BEING'

When asked which initiatives are crucial for organisations to promote emotional fitness, 45% responded: the work ambiance. This was revealed by the 'Global Wellbeing Survey 2022-2023'. Human resources leaders from more than a thousand organisations across all continents and in 46 countries participated in the survey. Organisations have a mission: to prioritise building a positive ambiance where well-being in all its facets is given a place. Corporate positivity as a method offers a solution here.

Well-being is a dynamic concept. It is constantly in motion. It depends on both internal and external factors, such as self-confidence, intrinsic motivation, recognition and appreciation, but also work pressure, hybrid working, and management. Well-being not only affects the people within organisations but also the quality of their performance. It is increasingly being integrated into general policy, no longer seen as a handful of individual programmes unrelated to the broader organisational narrative. As stated in the Global Wellbeing Survey 2022-2023: 'Wellbeing is (much!) more than a strategy of words and the occasional small gesture.'

Positive ambiance is one of the patterns of corporate positivity. If you want to move with and within your organisation towards a positive ambiance the following four habits are essential:

1. Energising people with positive interactions.
2. Being grateful and expressing it.
3. Contributing to a climate of trust.
4. Creating opportunities for enjoyment.

A FIRST HABIT: ENERGISING PEOPLE WITH POSITIVE INTERACTIONS

Below, we link providing people with energy through positive interactions to both giving, receiving, and measuring energy.

Energy resides throughout your body. Positive energy is characterised by a sense of being lively and excited, radiating vitality and flair. It enables us to perform, create, and persevere. Positive energy unlocks resources within us, the impact of which we barely understand. Energy is within you, within all of us, from top to bottom, from left to right. Kim Cameron (2012) states that we all possess three different types of energy that we must take care of. In this chapter, we further demonstrate how people give and receive energy uplifting one another through positive interactions.

Physical energy is associated with the interaction between glucose, the substance that provides energy for our cells, and adenosine triphosphate, a molecule produced by our cells that captures and delivers that energy where needed. Activity, whether it's a long, hard day or running a marathon, depletes the body of these substances. We need to recover through nutrition, relaxation, and sleep.

Mental energy is associated with concentration and cognitive focus. When we exert intense mental effort that requires prolonged concentration, we become mentally fatigued. Most of us have experienced being so tired that even thinking was difficult. Mental energy is recharged through mental breaks, relaxation, and by shifting focus to something light. Even while writing our book, we frequently needed to recharge our mental energy. A walk by the sea as a writing break, taking our eyes off the laptop and smartphone screens, a warm shower, and so on.

Emotional energy is associated with experiencing intense feelings. Just like physical and mental energy, we can also become exhausted from emotional energy. Think, for example, of the loss of a colleague, burnout, and so on. We need recovery to replenish this form of energy. Nowadays, everyone has a smartphone. Undoubtedly, you do too, and you recharge it. You find that completely normal. A metaphor clarifies. With a new smartphone, you probably notice that it's faster and the battery still works well. There's still enough memory. The more apps you install and the longer you use it, the slower the system becomes and the faster the battery drains. The same is true for us. If you've stored too many intense emotions, your 'system' slows down, you can do less with it, and your battery drains faster. You replace your smartphone after a few years, but your body and brain have to last a lifetime.

In addition to these three internal batteries, there is a fourth: relational energy, the energy you give to and receive from others. In contrast to the previous types of energy, which can deplete us when used excessively, Cameron asserts that expressing and receiving relational energy through positive interpersonal relationships elevates, stimulates, and rejuvenates us. It increases rather than decreases as it is used. Your energy is not diminished or depleted by the interaction; instead, it is renewed and amplified. Think, for instance, of friendship and support. They give you energy. Since delving into positive psychology, we have been more curious and captivated than ever by the insights into the power of relational energy. For us, it is a new dimension for creating depth in our collaboration with clients. When you expend physical, mental, and emotional energy, you need to 'recharge' yourself afterwards. When you give relational energy, you also receive it back from the other person. It is both generated and transferred weaving a powerful connection between everyone it touches.

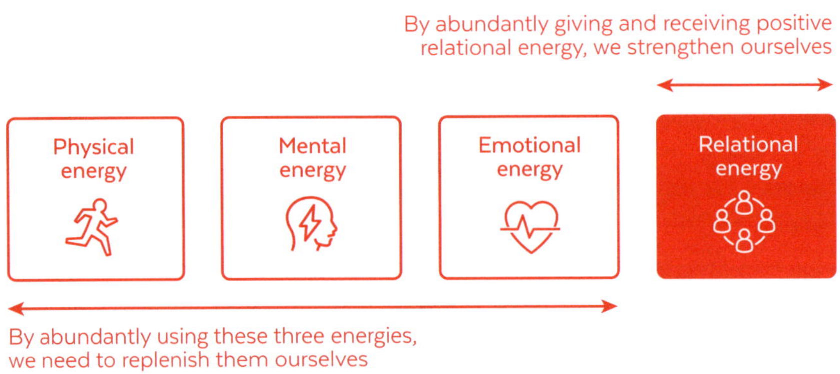

Figure 5. Different Types of Energy.

The workplace plays a central role in the lives of many people. We spend more time working than on any other daily activity. It is vital that individuals within every organisation feel connected and supported by colleagues and leaders. The well-being of organisations and their employees largely depends on the quality of interactions. These are seen, heard, and felt. The following case demonstrates this.

We are asked to listen to a team working in the social sector. The management team tells us that this team is underperforming, and they can't quite pinpoint the cause. When we meet the team, we are 'infected' with a negative energy field. There is complaining, a lot of negativity, reflections on how good things used to be. The team only sees problems, not solutions. It's incredible how deeply this can impact a person: resignation and cynicism can be heard, seen, and felt. The team cannot break

Patterns do not emerge suddenly. By agreeing to work on small habits to-gether, a positive movement is set in motion.

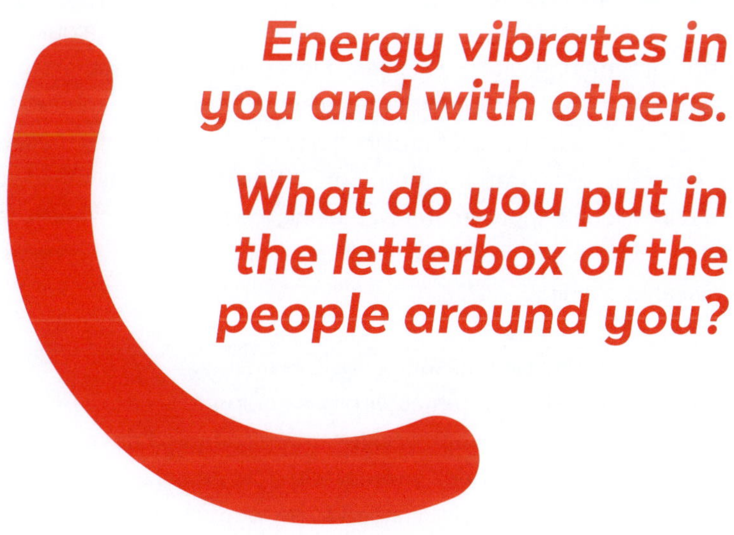

Energy and Motivation are not Synonyms

Motivation gets you moving. Energy, on the other hand, is something you transmit to and receive from others. It is common for organisations to provide context and resources to boost motivation. However, it is equally important to pay attention to ensuring an environment where positive relationships can occur. Anyone can be a positive energy giver, regardless of title or hierarchical position.

The Student as a Positive Energy Giver: A Criterion for Admission to the University of Michigan

Kim Cameron, Professor Emeritus of Management and Organisations at the University of Michigan, admits only students who are capable of transmitting positive energy to others into the university's academic department. This is even one of the key criteria for being allowed to pursue a doctorate. After twenty years of applying this criterion, it has resulted in a spectacularly high-performing, stimulating group of colleagues. To date, we have not found any comparable studies or cases in Europe.

Measuring is Knowing

Do you dare to measure the energy in your organisation? Positive energy can best be measured by asking individuals to what extent they personally gain energy from interacting with a colleague. Measuring energy is, therefore, an individual subjective assessment. In his research, Cameron and his team discovered five statements that provide reliable information for measuring positive energy in organisations (Cameron, 2013). The findings of his study reveal that individuals show greater well-being, job satisfaction, team cohesion, willingness to learn, creativity, results, and engagement when exposed to positive relationships.

Cameron's Statements for measuring positive energy:
- I feel invigorated when I interact with this person.
- After interacting with this person, I feel more energy to do my work.
- I feel increased vitality when I interact with this person.
- I would go to this person when I need to be "pepped up".
- After an exchange with this person, I feel more stamina to do my work.

There are various ways to map out positive networks. Here, we highlight three methods. First, you can investigate who within your organisation provides energy. Ask colleagues to write down the names of the three people who exude the most positive energy in the organisation. Tally up the results for each person. This helps to identify the energising employees in the organisation. Another method is to conduct a weekly survey asking employees to rate their energy levels on a scale of ten. Track the trend lines and plot the averages over time. The final method involves circulating an employee questionnaire about positive networks. Include the following questions:

- Who are the employees that spread the most positive energy?
- What are the three main characteristics of the people who give you the most energy?
- What do you need to enhance positive energy?
- What recognitions do we give to those who provide energy?
- How can we use mentoring to encourage pairs to stimulate each other's positive energy?
- What teams can we form to elevate positive energy to a higher level?
- What activities can we organise to promote positive energy in interpersonal relationships?
- To what extent do you consider the provision of positive energy a criterion for promotion?

A SECOND HABIT: BEING GRATEFUL AND EXPRESSING IT

Dear reader, what are your plans? How will you contribute to a positive ambiance by consciously focusing on gratitude, sincerely and from the heart of who you are? This is not a casual question. It is a call to action, no, more than a call to action. In this habit, we highlight the principle of gratitude. We discuss two studies on the impact of gratitude and present several options for mapping gratitude.

What follows are some practical tips for experimenting with gratitude.

- *Answer three questions daily:*
  - *What gratitude have I felt and expressed?*
  - *What have I given to others to be grateful for?*
  - *What difficulties have I caused that prevented gratitude from oc-curring?*
- *Keep a gratitude journal:*
  - *Write down a few things you are grateful for each morning or evening. A simple notebook or an app will suffice. Also, note why you are grateful for what you write down.*
- *Use reminders to be grateful: a background on your phone, a post-it on your laptop or in the car, a gadget in your handbag.*
- *Activate an app to meditate on gratitude.*
- *Create a gratitude wall with post-its.*
- *Engage your senses: Appreciate everything you can see, smell, taste, and hear.*
- *Use visual reminders to help you appreciate what you have.*
- *Seek out new moments and experiences to feel grateful.*

We can be grateful for small and big things, such as:
- A productive workday, a nice colleague, a new customer, a staff party, coffee and cake during a meeting, a cafeteria plan, hybrid working, attending events and webinars.
- Your partner and children, family, friends, a roof over your head, a warm shower.
- A new day, going outside without a coat, nature, inner strength, inspiration, a healthy body, peace, freedom, doing enjoyable things, having energy, healthy food.
- A good book, favourite music, your pet, a good night's sleep.

Gratitude works like a Magnifying Glass

Gratitude magnifies good things. It is a positive and reciprocal emotion we experience when something is good for ourselves or others. We can view it more broadly as the spontaneous tendency to appreciate the good in life. The Journal of Positive Psychology frequently publishes new studies on gratitude. From the early days of positive psychology, it has been one of the most researched topics. For a long time, the results from the studies were inconclusive. In recent years, many studies have been published that increasingly substantiate the impact of gratitude. Robert A. Emmons, the world's leading scientific expert on gratitude, proves that gratitude leads to greater well-being. Emmons' research shows that people who keep a gratitude journal significantly increase their well-being over time. He attributes this to the way it makes us focus on the positive instead of the negative. It helps us overcome our negativity bias, the natural tendency to remember negative experiences rather than positive ones (Emmons, 2008). Gratitude is both a state and a trait. It can arise from a situation, an event, or be part of your DNA.

More than just a 'Thank You'

What if we consider gratitude as a catalyst for a positive ambiance? Would we then aspire to be a grateful organisation? In Seligman's PERMA model (Seligman, 2012), which includes positive emotion, engagement, relationships, meaning, and accomplishment, gratitude is an important positive emotion. The effects of experiencing and expressing gratitude are endless. Gratitude impacts our emotional, psychological, and social well-being.

Research shows that where there is more attention to gratitude at work, this has positive effects on employees and organisations at various levels. Employees report experiencing less stress, feeling calmer, and feeling more connected to colleagues. They feel good and are happy to contribute to overall job satisfaction. Employees who experience gratitude perform better and exhibit social behaviour. Additionally, there is 'organisational citizenship behaviour': employees gladly and spontaneously do more than what is expected of them. A positive ambiance does not emerge spontaneously in the culture of organisations. It requires conscious action. Expressing and recognising gratitude is one of the levers for fostering that positive ambiance. We'd love to share a touching example from our practice.

Feeling gratitude and not expressing it is like wrapping a gift and not giving it.

Barometers for Gratitude

There are various questionnaires to measure gratitude. The most commonly used questionnaires are the GRAT ('Gratitude, Resentment and Appreciation Test') and the GQ-6 ('Gratitude Questionnaire'). Here, we present you with a sample of questions from the GRAT. This will help you grasp the full essence of gratitude.

Appreciation for others:
- I am where I am today thanks to the help of many others.
- Although I have control over my own life, I often think of the people who have supported and helped me.

Sense of abundance:
- Many good things have happened to me in my life.
- I have enough to live well, and I always get my fair share.

Simple pleasures:
- I often pause to think about what is good in my life.
- I thoroughly enjoy each day that I live.

 During our interventions, we specifically focus on gratitude. We often encounter scepticism and even disinterest. It is quickly viewed as something fluffy. However, we encourage you, dear reader, to answer the GRAT questionnaire with an open mindset. There are many things to be grateful for that we don't usually consider. We take them for granted.

Grateful Brains

Studies have shown that the brain functions differently in people who consciously reflect on things they are grateful for over a period of thirty days. Dr. Daniel G. Amen has taken brain scans of healthy individuals before and after they focused on gratitude for a few weeks. Certain limbic parts of their brains, such as the thalamus and the medial prefrontal cortex, were very active. The limbic parts associated with negative emotions, like the amygdala, were less active. Whether you're grateful for something that happened yesterday or twenty years ago—the positive effects remain (Amen, 2022).

What we think and consequently feel impacts what we want and do. Consciously thinking about things to be grateful for generates a positive emotion, prompting the move towards wanting and doing. For instance, you may be grateful for the constructive feedback you received from a colleague about a report. The feedback gives you a sense of pride. This leads you to spontaneously take on the next report. It is delightful that we too can receive gratitude for our expertise, enthusiasm, dedication, and optimism: a bouquet of flowers at the end of a project, a quote full of gratitude in the mailbox, thoughtful mentions on LinkedIn, a phone call about a success, a compliment.

A THIRD HABIT: CONTRIBUTING TO A CLIMATE OF TRUST

In this habit, we guide you from broad to narrow. We start with psychological safety, introduce an innovative method for trust-related conversations, and conclude with self-confidence. Amy Edmondson is an American scholar and professor at Harvard Business School. Her research area focuses on the impact of human interactions on success. She has conducted extensive research on the concept of psychological safety. According to Edmondson, psychological safety refers to our perception of how the group will react to us and our actions. Can I be myself? Am I allowed to speak up? Can I make mistakes? Can I take risks? (Edmondson, 2018). Consider, for example, your participation in a new project at work. You have an assignment, but you don't really understand why you were specifically asked to join the project. Do you ask about the clear end goal of the project? Do you openly question your role? Or do you fear this might come across as uninterested and avoid drawing attention to yourself?

Edmondson conducted extensive comparative research on the effectiveness of different teams. Her data shows that teams that make more mistakes but communicate about them are still more efficient than teams where making mistakes is not tolerated or discussed. Edmondson describes psychological safety as an environment where people can freely ask questions, share ideas, and provide feedback/feedforward. People are convinced that they will not be punished or humiliated for expressing ideas, questions, concerns, or mistakes. In such a team, it is safe to take interpersonal risks. Such an environment encourages people to be their authentic selves. Everyone is respected and valued. It is the ultimate prerequisite for trust, collective learning, creativity, innovation, engagement, and performance.

Psychological safety requires courage. It's not about being nice. It's about giving candid feedback, openly admitting mistakes, and learning from each other. A culture where this is possible is increasingly vital, yet misconceptions about psychological safety persist. We clear these up before bridging the gap from psychological safety to trust.

- **Myth 1:** Psychological safety is all about being nice and avoiding discomfort.
  Truth: Psychological safety gives team members the freedom to have tough, honest conversations and tackle difficult situations head-on.

- **Myth 2:** Psychological safety comes from the top.
  Truth: Psychological safety is 'hyper-local'. This means that every team member affects the sense of safety for those around them.

- **Myth 3:** Psychological safety is static.
  Truth: Psychological safety can be built up but can also diminish.

In creating a sense of safety it is important to be aware of our own actions. Every action we take sends a signal to the people around us. Building safety means being mindful of our signals and continually striving to strengthen the place of each member in the team. This is how psychological safety grows. We share three methods that we wholeheartedly support.

- 'Walking Conversations': a method to uncover and discuss confessions of distrust.
- 'Mistakes in the Spotlight': a way to experience that making mistakes is allowed in a climate of trust.
- 'Givers and Breakers': a paired walk using a set of cards.

'Walking Conversations' is a dialogue format where you engage in a conversation while walking through an empty space around a theme. This method allows different perspectives within a group to surface quickly. Everyone is actively involved in the conversation and it becomes immediately clear where everyone stands, both physically in the room and in their viewpoint. The method was actively used by Myrna Lewis in South Africa during the dismantling of apartheid. Nowadays, the Lewis method is used in many countries to dissolve polarities between people, give everyone a voice, and connect.

In 'Mistakes in the Spotlight', the focus is not on sharing successes. On the contrary, it deliberately highlights errors, mistakes, and failures. The added value of this method is multifaceted: it brings in new perspectives; it creates a strong connection; it creates a safe space where vulnerability has a place; it fosters responsibility, and it normalises failure. This allows for the creation of a more positive culture around failures.

Also, 'Givers and Breakers' is a method where movement is important. Participants start with a set of cards that list potential trust givers and breakers. While walking, they gain a better understanding of what is crucial for mutual trust. The cards with givers explain to the other person what is important for you to collaborate in trust: openly sharing information; daring to openly express what comes to mind; avoiding judgement; and so on. The cards with breakers indicate what the other person should definitely not do with you: not letting you finish speaking; withholding information; covering up mistakes; and so forth. By having these conversations while walking, you also avoid too direct and prolonged eye contact. Looking each other straight in the eyes can be threatening.

The Anatomy of Trust

The Dalai Lama said: 'Trust cannot be bought in the supermarket. You must possess it as a part of yourself.' The phrase shows that it is not always straightforward to make something tangible out of trust. Nevertheless, there are approaches that can help with this: what can you do to give and receive trust, in other words, to establish a climate of trust?

When conducting research on models of trust and building trust, you'll find quite a lot. It is a broad concept. Trust is the willingness to regard the other with positive intent. As soon as you sense that someone is wearing a mask, trust disappears. A meeting can take place in psychological safety. That does not mean that everyone in the room trusts each other. Even though we may know that sharing ideas openly is accepted, you can still lack trust in a colleague.

In our many years of experience with clients in all possible sectors, we have also experimented. We searched for the most applicable framework for trust. We do not hold the ultimate truth. Today, however, we do have a preference, namely Brené Brown's framework: 'BRAVING' (Brown, 2018). BRAVING describes seven clear pillars that together create trust. Brown also makes a strong link between trust and self-confidence. You can see the BRAVING tool as a guide for genuine conversations about trust, conversations between colleagues where curiosity, eagerness to learn, and trust have their place.

Feel free to try it out. Have a discussion with a colleague or your team about these seven pillars. You will notice that connection and trust will grow. This is essential for cultivating a positive ambiance.

1) *Boundaries*
   You respect my boundaries, and I respect yours. When it is unclear what is or isn't acceptable, we ask. We are also allowed to say no.

2) *Reliability*
   We do what we say we will do. We remain aware of our knowledge and abilities, but also our limitations. This way, we don't overpromise and can keep our promises.

3) *Accountability*
   We own our mistakes, apologise when necessary, and make amends.

4) *Vault*

   We do not share information or experiences that are not ours to share.

5) *Integrity*

   We choose courage over comfort; what is right over what is fun, fast, or easy. We translate our values into standards and concrete behaviour.

6) *Non-judgment*

   We can ask for what we need. We can talk about how we feel without judgment. We see asking for help as a sign of strength.

7) *Generosity*

   We interpret each other's intentions, words, and actions as generously as possible.

 We encourage translating this within teams and organisations on a deeper level. Agreements about trust can differ for each team. Taking the time to connect based on BRAVING, is a particularly powerful foundation for sustainable trust and a positive ambiance. You can find more about BRAVING on Brené Brown's website.

We are facilitating a team coaching session. The executive team of the organisation highlights a lack of trust between departments. They provide examples of where things have gone wrong within their teams. When the executive team, during a subsequent team coaching session, once again directs all their criticism towards their team members, we decide to confront them. In our view, it is not the teams, but the executives at the table who are responsible for the mistrust and the resulting conflict. We work on their mutual trust, or rather mistrust. By the end of the day, issues that have remained unspoken for months can finally be addressed. One executive tells a colleague that, in his perception, it is the colleague's

Nine times out of ten, when trust is broken, it's due to small things. It's the business as usual behaviour that people experience with each other every day. People don't intend to break trust. Yet they do, unintentionally, in the rush and pace of workload, constant change, targets, and deadlines. You do it. I do it. We all do it.

Self-Confidence

Confidence primarily concerns how we interact with others. However, the foundation of confidence lies in having self-confidence. Unfortunately, this is often the first thing to falter when we fail or feel disappointed. Conscious-ly or unconsciously, we question confidence in ourselves: 'It must be my fault.' Can you recall such a moment? Can you assess it against the BRAVING model?

- Did I respect my boundaries and was I clear about what is and isn't okay for me?
- Could I rely on myself or did I overpromise?
- Did I take responsibility or did I place the blame on others?
- Did I involve others who were not actually part of it?
- Did I have the courage to do the right thing or did I choose the eas-iest solution?
- Did I ask for help when needed? Did I condemn myself?
- Was I gentle enough with myself?

*Trust requires working
on self-confidence.*

*Trust is the adhesive
that holds teams and
organisations together.*

A FOURTH HABIT: CREATING OPPORTUNITIES FOR ENJOYMENT

We guide you towards enjoyment along the following path: the definition and misconception of enjoyment; pain and pleasure; ideas to involve everyone in experiencing enjoyment.

Enjoyment comes in all possible forms. This is evident from research. We can derive enjoyment from seeing a colleague again, closing a deal, or having a pleasant feedback conversation. We can also find enjoyment in taking revenge, making someone look ridiculous during a meeting, or in a colleague's poor results. Here lies a misconception about enjoyment. Enjoyment is often associated with living in excess, exuberant fun, and pleasant experiences. But it doesn't have to be. You can find enjoyment in five minutes of silence, having a constructive exit interview, or in memories of your deceased father. The definition is simple: enjoyment is what you find pleasurable.

Everything we do, according to Freud, is based on two fundamental needs: to avoid pain or to experience pleasure. This is known as the 'Pain Pleasure Principle'. Both needs are biologically driven and act as guiding forces in our lives. Before you undertake any action, you weigh up whether it is associated with pain or pleasure. Every decision we make is based on this principle, whether consciously or unconsciously. We are more influenced by pain than by pleasure. Pain is a stronger motivator than pleasure. We make more decisions to avoid pain than to seek pleasure.

Your colleague tells you she is going on a diet. When you ask her why, she says it is because she can no longer fit into her clothes. She doesn't mention that she longs to wear a short dress again. It has been proven that your colleague will be more successful with her diet if she focuses on the short dress she desires, rather than the trousers that no longer fit.

Your team member becomes anxious because a quote has not yet been sent out. This reaction is driven more by the fear of being seen as unprofessional than by the desire to work with the prospect in the future. We can consciously choose to focus on the pleasure (the short dress, the pleasant collaboration ‿) rather than the pain (the tight trousers and the poor image). It has been proven that this promotes action and change, leading to more sustainable results.

Joy Ignites Energy

Directly linking corporate profit to joy is a step too far. Nonetheless, we are convinced there is an indirect connection. In many organisations, deadlines overshadow the opportunity to experience joy. Work in that environment lacks any sense of 'play and joy'. Work is still something you simply do for eight hours a day. Other organisations excel at creating multiple opportunities for play, celebration, and enjoyment. They firmly believe that this improves relationships, enhances team spirit, and fosters a positive ambiance. During certain moments, there is no other official agenda, just joy for the sake of joy.

Ben & Jerry's Ice Cream has a permanent committee: the 'Joy Gang'. The Joy Gang has three tasks: planning fun activities for coworkers; awarding 'Joy Awards' worth 500 dollars for cheerful ideas that bring joy to the workplace; and organising annual events and competitions where fun is the central theme.

The benefits of a positive work environment for engagement, well-being, and productivity are well-known. Yet, many still feel uneasy about the concept of having fun at work. Their belief remains that fun is something that happens outside working hours, detracting from concentration and taking time away from our daily tasks.

That said, fostering fun in the workplace is important. Fun in the workplace is a significant factor in employee happiness. A sense of fun helps people have a more positive mindset, feel better, and think more positively. Organisations with higher levels of employee well-being, where fun is embraced, report lower levels of absenteeism, better productivity, and more energy. Fun is a fantastic way to foster better collaboration and communication within an organisation. Employees get to know each other better, understanding each other's strengths, weaknesses, and boundaries more effectively.

Make Room for Fun

What we must remember about fun is that it cannot be imposed; people need to be in the mood, which is difficult if they feel stressed, anxious, and exhausted at work. We all know the classics: the Friday afternoon drinks, the New Year's reception, the team-building outing, and so on. But there is so much more we can do to give fun a platform in organisations. It is the responsibility of human resources and managers to enforce this platform within the organisation and to build it. Only when people believe in the impact of a positive ambiance in the organisation do fun initiatives become enjoyable. Only when fun initiatives are established can the work ambiance truly evolve positively. We wish to highlight this interplay. Without it, the image of obligatory work outings, time-consuming and pointless activities, etc., quickly emerges.

Albert Einstein once said, 'Play is the highest form of research.' Dale Carnegie stated, 'People rarely succeed unless they have fun in what they are doing.' The Dutch cultural historian Johan Huizinga conducted extensive research on play and fun. He proposed that humans be called 'Homo Ludens' (playful human) instead of 'Homo Sapiens' (wise human). Huizinga posits that 'civilization arises and unfolds in and as we play'. We assert that there is still a child within each of us. That it is time to reintegrate the child, within ourselves, in life, but certainly also in the business world. As organisational experts, we consistently experiment with moments of fun in our projects, consciously and deliberately but without obligation. Carlos, in the case below, has also taken a few steps.

We are facilitating a leadership development programme in an international organisation. We have a lively debate about the behavioural indicators outlined in their leadership model. The competence 'enable', also includes 'providing time for creativity and fun.' Some find this challenging. Carlos, too, is convinced that his team does not value this, or worse, finds it ridiculous. For him, it does not fit within the organisation's culture. However, Carlos is willing to take a small step. Dancing on stage isn't quite his thing. Bringing homemade tapas on a Friday afternoon for a moment of togetherness with the team, that he is happy to commit to. His decision stems more from 'pain' than 'pleasure', but he is still willing to give it a try. We meet again a month later in the next workshop. Carlos has brought homemade snacks. He wants to thank the group by letting them experience how delightful such an unguarded, surprising moment can be. We reflect on this moment: what a beautiful breakthrough.

Positive interactions, gratitude, trust, enjoyment. These are the matters discussed in this chapter. They might not yet be established habits in your organisation. Perhaps they are perceived as somewhat 'fluffy'. However, they are essential for creating a positive ambiance. They contribute to flourishing at various levels, as we outlined at the beginning in our definition of positive psychology: emotional, psychological, and social well-being.

Don't concern yourself with major changes, instead start with a small habit.

CONNECTION

WITHOUT CONNECTION NO HARMONY

When Peterson, one of the founders of positive psychology, was asked what positive psychology is all about in a few words, he said, 'Other people matter.' Positive connection in life does not happen in isolation. As humans, we are fundamentally connected to other people. Philosophy and religion have pointed out for centuries that it is only possible for individuals and groups to flourish in the presence of positive relationships.

Organisations have the duty to create a context where positive connections can occur. The wonderful news is that everyone within organisations can cultivate habits that nurture and strengthen these connections. Positive psychology provides us with interesting perspectives to establish connections in a powerful way.

Positive connection is one of the patterns of corporate positivity. If you want to move towards positive connection with and within your organisation, the following four habits are essential:

1. Seeing, hearing, and feeling qualities.
2. Stimulating making the most of qualitiess.
3. Connecting with the head and the heart.
4. Supporting in both positive and negative situations.

A FIRST HABIT: SEEING, HEARING, AND FEELING QUALITIES

In this habit, we explore the concept of 'qualities': discovering and articulating your own qualities; creating connection by learning to see and name the qualities in others.

We all have qualities. Linley et al. demonstrated that people who make greater use of their qualities score higher on self-confidence, experience of competence, achievement of goals, and sense of well-being (Linley et al., 2010). Qualities are part of who we are. The beauty of qualities is that they can be discovered, practiced, and developed. All qualities are positive and can strengthen and complement each other. Working with qualities increases motivation and energy because we operate based on who we are.

Whether it concerns guiding learning processes, individual or team coaching, mentoring, or positive peer reviews, we always and consistently work with the qualities of our clients. We have crafted a range of tools to support this. In the following case, we used our colourful qualities cards.

During a coaching session, Aisha shares that she finds it difficult to name her own qualities. Using our qualities cards, Aisha comes to realise that she can spontaneously identify with about five qualities. She is realistic, thinks critically, is loyal, caring, and driven. She just found it hard to put these qualities into words.

From our expertise, we would like to offer two concrete suggestions to work with your qualities: learning to articulate your qualities and mapping them out. You might be triggered to map out your qualities, but you need to be able to express them in words. During our interventions, we frequently discover that this is not as straightforward as it seems. Check with yourself if you can spontaneously bring words to a quality present in the following scenarios.

- *You always see a solution. People come to you when they have a difficult problem. Your clear insight makes it seem like problems are easily solvable. Your incisive analysis always gets to the heart of the matter. You really are .... Did you immediately have a word for this quality? How about 'sharp-witted'?*

- *You can explain things so clearly. Others use twice as many words, but it's never as clear as when you do it. You really are .... Ever considered 'to the point' as a quality?*

- *You weigh and consider things. Not too much, not too little. You balance examining the arguments but still come to a conclusion. Isn't it nice that you are so ....? What do you think of 'well-considered'?*

What characterises us and the people around us? Seeing, hearing, and feeling qualities requires a proactive attitude. It's not about one action we undertake. Collective actions can help us create a clearer picture of our identity. What comes next supports you in uncovering your unique qualities.

- Register your strengths. Pay attention to what goes well in your life, what doesn't need to change, or even must not change. How do you achieve this? What qualities do you bring to the table for this?
- Put modesty aside. What do you like or love about yourself? What makes it enjoyable to work with you? When are you cheerful, friendly, proud? What do others appreciate in you? What do you receive compliments for? What are you good at?
- Open the jar. What was your last success? What did you do? When did you overcome a difficult event? How did you manage that? What do you find important?
- Look at yourself through a positive lens. What was your contribution to your success and/or that of your team, your organisation? What comes easily to you, while others find it more difficult? How do you quickly come up with good ideas?
- Tell who your hero is. Who inspires you? Who has played an important role in your life? Why?
- Identify your qualities. Analytical, calm, careful, caring, cautious, cheerful, concise, confident, consistent, courageous, creative, curious, decisive, diplomatic, disciplined, down-to-earth, driven, eager to learn, empathetic, enthusiastic, flexible, friendly, generous, good listener, grateful, helpful, honest, hopeful, humble, humorous, independent, intelligent, loving, loyal, modest, obedient, optimistic, patient, perceptive, persuasive, powerful, precise, punctual, realistic, receptive, reliable, reserved, responsible, sensitive, social, spiritual, team-oriented, thoughtful, tolerant, and so on.

Throughout our careers, we have always worked in learning environments ⌣. This has given us a vivid insight of the positive power of working with strengths. Strengths create a positive connection with ourselves and others. They promote well-being, motivation, and energy. They bring out the best version in people. Seeking out strengths is essential, both for yourself and your environment.

Difference between Qualities, Competencies, Interests, and Resources

Qualities

When we talk about qualities, we are referring to you. What makes you unique? What can you always rely on? Perseverance, honesty, drive, eagerness to learn, curiosity, or something else? At present, there is no universally accepted classification system for personal qualities. This is due to the ongoing development of vocabulary in this area. However, there are several valuable assessment methods that map personal qualities: The VIA Institute and Gallup are the most relevant for us:
- www.viacharacter.org
- www.gallup.com

Competencies

A competency is something you learn. Think, for example, of presenting, mastering a new IT system, leading a meeting.

Interests

Interests are subjects you are passionate about. Think, for instance, of learning & development, sustainability, and so forth.

Resources

When qualities are supported by external factors, such as the work environment, family, friendships, volunteer work, and so on, we talk about resources.

In our roles as organisational experts, coaches, and trainers, we encounter HR experts almost daily. We certainly do not wish to generalise, but we observe that in many companies across various sectors today, the focus still primarily lies on competencies, competency matrices, competency profiles, attitude, and so on. Competencies and attitude are undoubtedly important. We need competencies, attitude, and qualities. We have conducted extensive research into how to empower people in a professional context using their qualities. Recognising qualities in others can only happen when you ask yourself what that person brings to you, what you truly feel in the interaction. What is the positive experience that the person evokes in you? When someone acts in harmony with their own qualities, a powerful energy flow is ignited.

Olivia arrives at her coaching appointment visibly upset. She shares what happened to her that morning. Her little daughter woke up with a cold and couldn't go to daycare. Olivia couldn't leave for the office until her mother arrived to babysit. Olivia missed her train and arrived half an hour late. We hear the entire story, responding with empathy as we attentively listen to her account. We consciously look for her strengths. We see anxiety in her eyes. We hear concern in her voice. We share with her the qualities we observe, hear, and feel: care and a sense of responsibility. It's lovely to see. Her anxiety dissipates. It's not about the story Olivia shares. It's about what happens when she tells it. This nuance ensures that we consciously recognise her strengths and empower her, rather than focusing on limitations. Our clients smile, enjoy themselves, and feel eager for more whenever we discuss strengths. Everyone wants to know what truly defines them and what they can do with this knowledge.

The Power of the Here and Now

In our coaching practice, utilising a strength-based methodology, we observe that people often rush from one thing to another. The rapid pace of change exacerbates this behaviour. We all strive to meet expectations at home and at work. We draw information from the past and seek solutions for the future. Consequently, our focus easily shifts to what we have done and what we need to do, rather than on the qualities we possess as individuals to achieve these goals. As coaches, our full attention is on the present, much more than on the future or the past. Focusing on experiences in the here and now brings them to life and adds emotional intensity. It is precisely in the here and now that qualities can be discovered.

Becoming an Expert in Hearing, Seeing, and Feeling Qualities

We would like to offer you some advice. Empower your colleague when engaging in conversation. When people are close to their strengths, you can see and hear various things happening. Paying conscious attention to this allows you to discover, name, and reflect these qualities back. For example, when someone speaks in metaphors, it might indicate they are close to a strength. It is worthwhile to share your observation and inquire about it. What you might hear, see, and feel when the other person is stepping into his strength.

- Changing intonation.
- Varying voice volume.
- Speaking with great focus.
- Relaxed yet energetic.
- Greater sense of confidence.
- Use of words or phrases such as: 'Fantastic', 'Great', 'Incredible', 'I love that', and so on.
- More hand gestures, more movement.
- More metaphors.
- Completely absorbed in the story.
- Very detailed descriptions of successes.
- Bigger eyes.
- Radiant smile.
- Sitting up straight, surging upward.

You will find that the interplay of all qualities together impacts everyone's energy. Simply by reading this chapter, we set you in motion. We guarantee that something will happen to you during your next interaction. You will become aware of the qualities of others. The strength lies in providing feedback about this. Feedback that gives wings. Feedback that empowers people and fosters positive connections.

Qualities and Positive Psychology

In positive psychology, qualities hold a significant place in contemporary research. Identifying, naming, better understanding, effectively using personal qualities, setting developmental goals, and optimally developing these qualities are keys to flourishing. This concept dates back to ancient times. Aristotle spoke about it in the fourth century BC. To lead a good life, he suggested, 'we must strive to live in accordance with the best within us'. Clear and concrete empirical knowledge is available regarding the functioning of qualities. Qualities lead to better functioning and greater well-being, even in the long term.

Alex Linley researched the extent to which we utilise our strengths. The results showed that people who make greater use of their strengths scored higher on self-confidence, the experience of competence, goal achievement, and well-being. Other research also demonstrates that consciously using strengths correlates with increased engagement, autonomy, self-confidence, intrinsic motivation, and reduced absenteeism.

We strongly believe that the potential within an organisation becomes visible and grows when working with qualities. Research shows that employees want to grow in who they are, not just in what they know and can do. Qualities are a part of that.

As corporate positivity activists, we are trendsetters in fully embracing qualities to achieve results.

A SECOND HABIT: ENCOURAGING AND UTILISING STRENGTHS

There is a wealth of potential in every organisation. When people have a clear view of their strengths, they gain a boost of energy and willpower. It connects them with confidence, making it easier to achieve goals. Being reminded of what you or others possess builds trust and bridges the gap between past successes and future possibilities. In this chapter, you will discover how to build and optimally utilise your house of strengths.

Language Brings Life

As previously mentioned, we are not strong in articulating qualities: we lack a rich vocabulary. There is a biological explanation for this: our negativity bias. In other words, we tend to focus on the negative rather than the positive. We are quicker to notice what is going wrong than what is going right. We remember criticism better than compliments. Our attention is more easily drawn to negative rather than positive information. The explanation is evolutionary. Long ago, our ancestors were exposed to numerous life-threatening situations: predators, food shortages, and so on. Paying attention to negative stimuli played a useful role in survival.

The 'chance of not surviving' is no longer a direct threat for most of us. However, the connection in our brains is still made. Articulating qualities generates positive emotions. These enable us to function better, to flourish more. This, in turn, provides more strength to let go of negativity and to see and utilise qualities. When we name something, give it a label, we give it attention. We can then classify it, understand it, and relate it to other things. Without a label, these unknown words merely float on loose sand. They become lost. They are forgotten. The same applies to qualities. Aristotle has been quoted before: everything you give attention to grows.

We previously invited you to map out your own qualities using various methods and techniques. Can you now also spontaneously name the qualities of the people you work with? Let's list them again.

Analytical, calm, careful, caring, cautious, cheerful, concise, confident, consistent, courageous, creative, curious, decisive, diplomatic, disciplined, down-to-earth, driven, eager to learn, empathetic, enthusiastic, flexible, friendly, generous, good listener, grateful, helpful, honest, hopeful, humble, humorous, independent, intelligent, loving, loyal, modest, obedient, optimistic, patient, perceptive, persuasive, powerful, precise, punctual, realistic, receptive, reliable, reserved, responsible, sensitive, social, spiritual, team-oriented, thoughtful, tolerant, and so forth.

The House of Qualities

Qualities are situated at different levels. People are well aware of some of their qualities. Of others they are less or not at all aware. Nevertheless, they are also part of who they are. Everyone has different levels of qualities, ranging from highly visible to those that are more hidden. A key principle in positive psychology is that qualities are always available. They are part of our DNA. It is therefore worthwhile to visualise them in a house of qualities, from its foundations to the roof. This brings energy. In our activities with our clients, we notice a lack of practical ways to do this. Yet, the solution is simple. The exercise we share here is purely based on experience: building a house of qualities, as shown below in figure 6, and concretely identifying what the employee can do to use them more and more broadly. This can be done by having them visually at hand: a set of quality cards, quality stickers, a quality cloud, visual materials, and so on.

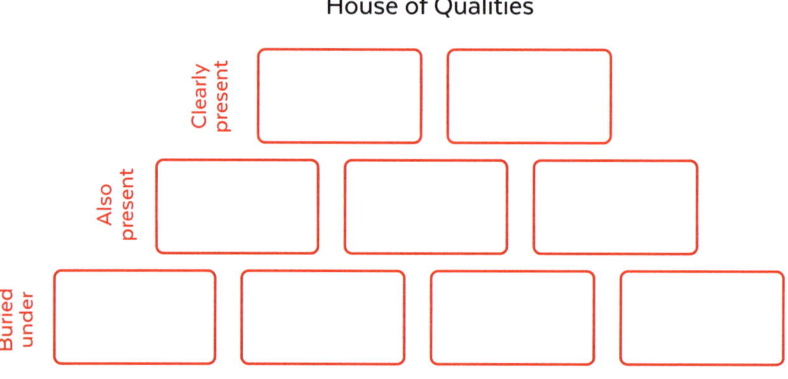

Figure 6. Example of a House of Qualities.

Qualities are Only Qualities when They are Utilised

But how do you translate that knowledge into behaviour? How can you apply qualities more broadly or differently? When you achieve this, you become more passionate about your work, gain more confidence in your abilities, and perform better. In other words, you let your qualities flourish. There are two approaches: discovering new applications where your qualities can also be utilised; and finding ways to make better use of your qualities in an existing context.

The golden rule, as researched by Alex Linley, is to utilise the right quality, in the right 'dose', in the right way, and at the right time (Linley, 2008). Too much of a good thing is not sustainable. Humour is a wonderful quality. However, if someone continuously trivialises the results with humour during a data meeting, that quality is not being used to its full potential. Using qualities at the wrong moment is also not a good option. Applying analytical thinking in an initial brainstorm about a new strategy hinders creativity.

Now is the time to shift towards a different way of collaborating. A collaboration that does not start from rational job descriptions with areas of responsibility, titles, departments, and tasks in rigid templates. A collaboration that is also open to job crafting and job carving: creating or adjusting jobs tailored to what makes someone unique.

A THIRD HABIT: CONNECTING WITH THE HEAD AND THE HEART

Our brain is an incredibly fascinating organ. Everything we do, think, feel, and experience resides within our brains. This allows us to always make choices. We can cope with all circumstances. Life doesn't have to be about fear and half-measures or 'what if' and regret. If we find the key to our brain, we live fully. In this chapter, we present some facts about the brain and its neuroplasticity. From there, we link to the connection between head and heart, and to positive emotions. We discuss the 'broaden-and-build' theory and the usefulness of negative emotions. Mindfulness and meditation are also briefly covered. But first, we briefly describe what our brain actually is.

The Netherlands Institute for Neuroscience provides impressive figures. Our brains weigh one to one and a half kilos, slightly more in women than in men ︶. By comparison, our skin weighs twice as much. Despite their weight, our brains use only 20% of our oxygen. In 13 milliseconds, the brain determines whether we find someone attractive or not. Our brain cells communicate at a speed of no less than 431 km/h. We make more than 10 million (micro) decisions per day, 95% of which are made unconsciously. Do I take coffee or tea at the machine? Do I turn the lights on or not? Do I take a second serving of lunch? Do I take a break now or later?

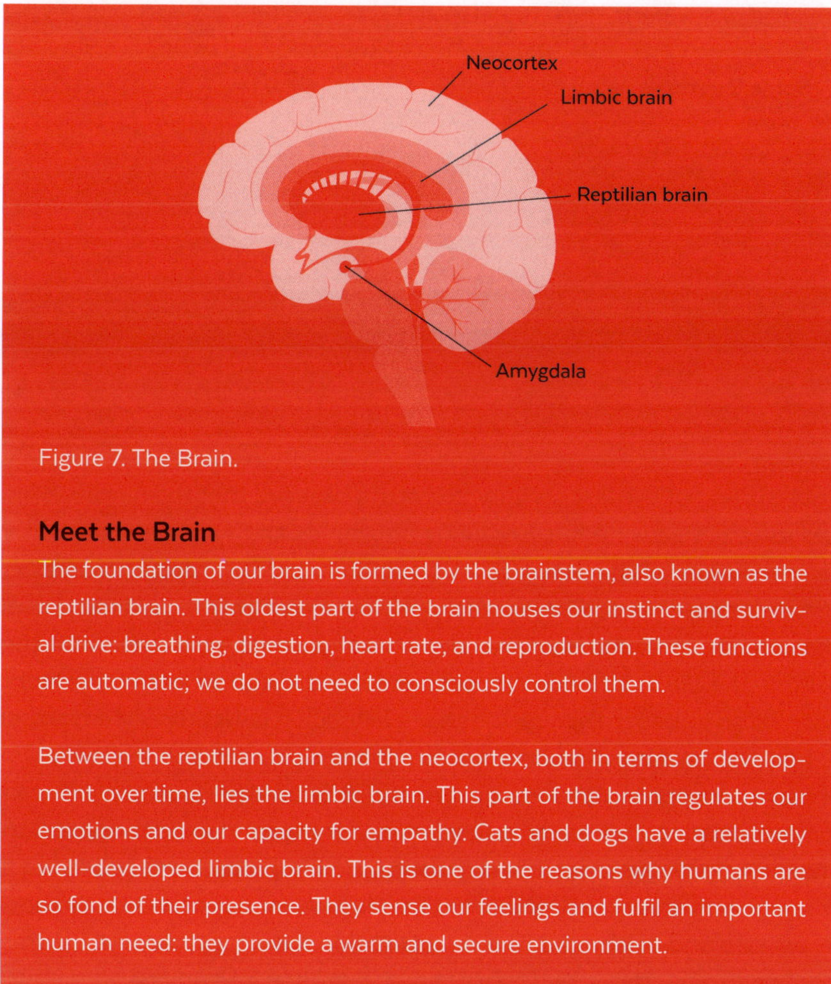

Figure 7. The Brain.

Meet the Brain

The foundation of our brain is formed by the brainstem, also known as the reptilian brain. This oldest part of the brain houses our instinct and survival drive: breathing, digestion, heart rate, and reproduction. These functions are automatic; we do not need to consciously control them.

Between the reptilian brain and the neocortex, both in terms of development over time, lies the limbic brain. This part of the brain regulates our emotions and our capacity for empathy. Cats and dogs have a relatively well-developed limbic brain. This is one of the reasons why humans are so fond of their presence. They sense our feelings and fulfil an important human need: they provide a warm and secure environment.

The neocortex enables us to think, process data, read, and write. Language resides in the neocortex. It houses all the skills that distinguish us from reptiles and other mammals.

The amygdala, located just in front and above the brainstem, is part of the limbic brain. Fear, danger, and stress can cause an overactive amygdala, which triggers certain reactions. In situations perceived as life-threatening, this part of our brain takes action. For our ancestors, these were mainly dangerous animals. Today, different factors come into play: transformation, workload, digitisation, and so on. What does the reptilian brain do when threatened by these situations? Fight, flight, or freeze.

Some Examples
Fight: You receive harsh criticism via email and immediately send a retaliatory response.

Flight: You are confronted with yet another change in strategy. You remain indifferent and let it slip by.

Freeze: You are 'attacked' in a meeting. You are stunned. You remain silent.

The Brain is Flexible

Until the end of the last century, scientists believed that the human brain and its structure were formed during pregnancy and fully developed after early childhood. They assumed that the brain hardly changed thereafter and even deteriorated. The connections were already made, and the brain's learning and growth period was over. Nothing could be further from the truth. In the 1980s and 1990s, neuroscientists discovered interesting facts. They found evidence that our brains are neuroplastic. Neuroplasticity refers to both the creation of new brain cells, known as neurons, and the formation of new connections via neurotransmitters between these neurons. Thanks to neuroplasticity, we are able to learn new things and adapt to new situations and environments. The popularisation of neuroscience has led to a greater interest in brain knowledge. The findings of neuroscience are now recognised and celebrated. They shed light on the possibilities we have as humans to grow, thrive, and connect with ourselves and others.

Head and Heart

"This is who I am, I'm not going to change anymore." If you think that way, it's time to stop it. We can influence our brain, fortunately . Moreover, we can influence our behaviour and emotions. What we think has a significant impact on what we feel, want, and do. Emotions are not just in our head. They are present throughout our body. We can invite emotions to the table when we long for connection. Connecting with head and heart can be learned.

Sophia is a true thinker. She seeks a rational explanation for everything. During one of our peer review sessions, it emerges that the collaboration with the purchasing department is not going smoothly. Sophia tells the team that she finds the purchasing department very strict with suppliers. She has charted the rejected discount rates to back up her opinion. During the peer review session, we encourage her to express how this affects her. The question surprises her. She cannot immediately answer. She continues with her reasoning. We explicitly ask her to name what she feels. She still finds this a difficult question. At that moment, we suggest several emotions: anger, nervousness, discomfort. She now indicates that she is worried. Sophia is now in touch with her feelings. We make the shift from head to heart, to what she truly wants. She desires a closer collaboration where everyone has a say. This would give her peace of mind. Sophia is willing to discuss this with the purchasing department.

The 'Broaden-and-Build' Theory

It is relatively recent that psychologists realised positive emotions are valuable in their own right. The person behind this realisation is Barbara Fredrickson, who has devoted most of her academic career to understanding the benefits of positive emotions (Fredrickson, 1998). What is their contribution, aside from feeling good? According to Fredrickson's 'broaden-and-build' theory, positive emotions encourage open, tolerant, and constructive thinking. Positive emotions thus create an opportunity for growth, broadening your thought and behaviour repertoire. When experiencing positive emotions, you are empathetic, flexible, and creative. It also leads to building new patterns: growing in new relationships, finding new approaches to old methods, and feeling good. Positive and negative emotions differ in their action tendencies. Negative emotions lead to narrowed behaviour, while positive emotions lead to broadened behaviour. We ourselves are great admirers of Barbara Fredrickson. In the video linked here, she gently explains the impact of positive emotions.

If you want to evoke positive emotions, we have tips for you.

- *Seek Connection*
  - *Think of a way to restore or strengthen a relationship with a colleague who has been out of sight for a while.*
  - *Call someone you should have called a long time ago.*
  - *Do something that involves meeting new people.*
  - *Work on connections at work.*
  - *Greet three people a day whom you don't know.*

- *Gossip Positively*
  - *Positive gossip involves sharing the qualities and successes of others. This positive image implicitly influences your colleague's relationship with others.*

- *Surprise*
  - *Do something unexpectedly positive for a colleague. Consider the difference this makes in your relationship with that colleague.*

- *Turn on the Positive Button*
  - *Take a moment to look at positive things around you. It doesn't matter where you are.*

Personal Growth and Development

Positive emotions broaden our attention, thinking, and actions. When we experience joy or interest, for example, we become more creative, see more opportunities, and are more open to relationships with others. Positive emotions also undo negative emotions. It is difficult to experience both positive and negative emotions simultaneously. Gentleness, joy, and contentment can relieve stress. Positive emotions also increase resilience. Pleasure, satisfaction, friendship, love, and affection all strengthen resilience. In this way, we build psychological 'reserves'. We can more easily withstand a figurative 'push'.

Positive Impact of Negative Emotions

We cannot make ourselves feel a certain emotion, nor can anyone implant them in us. They depend on our interpretations. Positive emotions contribute to our well-being, but this does not render negative emotions irrelevant or unimportant. It might sound strange, but negative emotions can have a positive effect. Negative emotions can lead to personality changes, such as during job loss, divorce, or illness. They can connect us with who we aspire to be and who we wish to avoid being. Negative emotions teach us to be more compassionate towards what happens in both our personal and professional lives.

Emotions are not like the weather; they do not just happen to us. Their influence is far greater than we realise. Our way of thinking and the meaning we assign to situations are hugely determining factors for our emotions. Positive emotions are like nutrients for growth. To stay physically and mentally healthy, a daily dose of positive emotions is just as important as exercising, eating vegetables, and fruit. In fact, we should all have a 'to feel list' alongside our to-do list.

For us, corporate positivity activists, consciously seeking out positive emotions is like having music throughout the day.

It goes without saying that emotions impact those around us. Emotions broadcast themselves. They inhabit our entire body. They are like a radio station that reaches many people, operating on all frequencies. Therefore, seeking out positive emotions is important for connecting with both yourself and others. It's good to know that to maintain a healthy balance, we need three positive emotions, events, or experiences for every negative emotion we experience.

Mindfulness and Meditation: A Source of Well-being

There is already a wealth of fascinating literature on mindfulness and meditation. There are also many tools and apps that can guide you in these practices. It is impossible not to mention them when discussing connecting with the head and the heart. We encourage you to explore this topic in depth. Meditation and mindfulness—people often use these terms interchangeably, and their goals seem similar. Both aim to reduce stress and increase enjoyment of life. However, there is a difference.

The goal of meditation is to focus your attention on the here and now and become aware of the thoughts that flit through your mind. You do nothing with these thoughts, other than try to let them go. Meditation is the practice of attention. There are many different ways to meditate. For instance, there is breathing meditation, where all your attention and concentration is focused on your breathing. There is also the body scan, where you pay attention to all parts of your body. This creates a feeling that can be described as silence, peace, and happiness. Just as your body needs rest to recover after exercise, so do your mind and thoughts. Meditating is just like resting.

A meditative walk differs from an ordinary walk. You consciously focus on nature and the smallest details in your body.

- *Walk, if possible, barefoot on the grass.*
- *Put your phone aside.*

Jon Kabat-Zinn is the founder of mindfulness (Kabat-Zinn, 1979). Mindfulness also revolves around attention, but to what you are doing in that present moment, in the here and now. Suppose you are drinking a cup of coffee, then you keep your attention on that coffee. The taste, the pleasant smell of it. You are not occupied with other things at the same time. Or if you are, for example, driving to the office, you don't think about the things you still need to do after your drive. You focus on the sounds around you, the feel of the steering wheel in your hand, and other things 'in the now'. Mindfulness is about applying attention, being fully engaged with what you are doing at that moment, and enjoying that moment without worrying. According to Jon Kabat-Zinn, mindfulness trains your brain and helps to structure your thoughts. This, in turn, would lead to an improvement in your well-being.

'Wherever you go, there you are.'

JOHN KABAT-ZINN

A FOURTH HABIT: SUPPORTING IN POSITIVE AND NEGATIVE SITUATIONS

In this paragraph, we guide you to explore and experiment with challenging your judgements and consciously choosing curiosity. We also provide a guide for step-by-step supportive communication in both positive and corrective situations.

The traditional Japanese tea room is entered through a door so small that you can only enter by crawling, regardless of your rank, function, or position. Inside the tea room, everyone is equal. Everyone looks out for each other and considers one another. Everyone is attentive and grateful for what is shared. Four basic principles serve as a guide: harmony, respect, purity, and tranquility. They offer a simple framework for relationships, both in positive connections and when there is a disagreement.

We all have a mental map. This map has been shaped by our age, experiences, religion, place of residence, upbringing, education, traumas and successes, genetic material, and so on. Everyone's mental map is unique and constantly evolving. This map forms our frame of reference. It filters how we view the world. It also determines the biases and prejudices we hold. We judge all day long. We cannot not judge. And we do it very quickly, don't we? When we meet someone for the first time, the first five seconds are crucial. We have already formed our judgement about that person. Judging is simply human. You will discover this in the video linked by the QR code.

We have met many leaders and employees who indicate that they find it difficult to avoid biases, judgements, and prejudices. This concerns us. Do you also face colleagues who judge or condemn? When working together, we want to avoid unfounded judgements based on incomplete information. Yet it happens. We generalise, forget to nuance. When we are stuck in a judgement, we cannot be supportive, whether in a positive or negative situation.

A supportive and connecting attitude only emerges when, at the moment of judgement, we shift to interest, curiosity, openness to the thoughts and world of the other. We warmly invite you to intentionally explore the mental landscape of another. Are you open to exploring the paths you might find there? Give it a try. Find a colleague who holds different opinions on certain topics. Enter the conversation with a healthy dose of openness and curiosity.

If we want to avoid quick judgements or prejudices, it helps to be consciously curious. Look at children. We can learn so much from them. They love to ask 'why'. They ask millions of questions to find out who you are and listen very attentively to what you say. We do not need to have all the answers either. As long as we ask questions out of genuine curiosity.

Curiosity and non-judgment are habits we can practise. When information reaches us, a judgment quickly follows. Can you recall a recent judgment you made? Below, you will find a thought process that helps foster curiosity about your colleague.

1) Think of a recent judgment: what were your thoughts?
'During the meeting last week, it crossed my mind that Max really likes to be in the spotlight.'

2) Recall the situation as detailed as possible: what actually happened?
'He asked to speak and explained his successful sale.'

3) Challenge your own judgment: 'How can I view this differently?'
'I could have thought that Max simply finds it important for us to share sufficiently within the team.'

4) Think of an argument that supports your judgment.
'My judgment stems from the fact that I personally do not find it appropriate to be in the limelight.'

5) Think of an argument that supports the other judgment.
'Max's motivation might be that he truly values sharing within the team.'

6) Check if you have enough facts to support your judgment.
'I am basing my judgment not on facts, but on interpretation.'

7) Check if there are reasons to accept another judgment.
'I have every reason to be open to another judgment. It can also enrich my perspective on the matter.'

Supportive Communication

We are ardent fans of Marshall Rosenberg's nonviolent communication (Rosenberg, 2011). In our many interactions, we notice that while the model is often known, it is rarely actively used. We are not born with the gift of good communication; it is a language we can learn. Rosenberg developed a communication method based on equality and empathy to build relationships that meet everyone's needs. To achieve this, connection is essential: connection with yourself and the other person, with desires and needs. The method consists of three processes: self-empathy, honest expression, and empathy. Here, we focus on the second process, where you convey a message to another person in an honest and connecting way. A connecting communication always includes four components:

- Observe without judging
- Feel rather than think
- Express needs rather than actions
- Make requests rather than demands

Do Not Judge, Observe

Can we avoid expressing judgments in communication?

- Present facts: what you hear, see, read, learn.
- Present the facts without judgment.
- Avoid assumptions and generalisations.
- Clarify your personal interpretations with facts.

A few examples make this concrete:

- A judgment: "You are not discreet."
  An observation: "I hear that you shared some confidential matters discussed in the meeting. Personally, I find that indiscreet."

- A judgment: "Aline is a weak project manager."
  An observation: "Aline has not completed the past projects within the scheduled deadlines."

Do Not Think, Feel

In our roles as coaches, trainers, and organisational experts, we encounter a fear of emotions almost daily. We are not accustomed to expressing our emotions. We often struggle to connect with our feelings and have a limited emotional vocabulary. Expressing vulnerability is still taboo in many organisations. Expressing and naming emotions requires courage in organisational culture. It is essential for effective communication to know how we feel and to articulate it. Naming our feelings, in all our vulnerability, fosters connection. You connect with your own feelings to be able to connect with others from that place. Our daily practice clearly shows that there is still much work to be done in this area. As authors, we see it as our duty to emphasise the importance of this. By expanding the vocabulary of specific emotions, we deepen our connections with each other and provide support.

Positive Emotions

Accepted, at ease, blissful, calm, carefree, cheerful, comfortable, competent, confident, connected , content, encouraged, energetic, enjoyable, enthusiastic, familiar, grateful, happy, hopeful, in love, inspired, joyful, loved, motivated, peaceful, pleasant, proud, relaxed, relieved, safe, strong, tranquil, valuable.

Negative Emotions

Afraid, angry, annoyed, anxious, ashamed, betrayed, bored, conflicted, confused, dependent, depressed, desperate, disappointed, discouraged, dissatisfied, empty, enraged, frustrated, furious, hostile, humiliated, hurt, impatient, insecure, jealous, lost, mad, nervous, panicked, powerless, used, rejected, rushed, sad, shameful, shocked, shy, sorrowful, stressed, tense, threatened, useless, weak, worried.

No Action but a Need

Why do we feel a certain way? The search for the answer to this question brings us to our needs. A need is not something we want; it is neither an action nor a plan. A need is what we require from within ourselves to answer the questions: 'Why do I feel this way? What do I find important?' Needs stem from values. This is why we can understand them and connect to them. Actions, on the other hand, are ways to fulfil our needs. Here are some examples of needs and their requests for an action.

- I need contact. I would like to propose scheduling a weekly check-in.
- I need trust. I wanted to know if you're okay with working with a shared calendar.
- I need a new challenge. I wanted to ask if you could involve me in the new project.

Needs

A challenge, a goal, a role model, being heard, calm, care, clarity, collaboration, comfort, communication, contact, contributing, creativity, equality, freedom, friendship, help, honesty, information, inspiration, learning, movement, openness, order, providing help, recognition, respect, safety, self-confidence, silence, simple things, space, stability, structure, support, time, trust, understanding.

Not a Demand but a Request

A request is only strong when it is made in a connecting manner. It is not a demand. It is a concrete question for a feasible solution, positively phrased: what we desire rather than what we would avoid. If we make connected communication a habit, we can fully embrace who we are, with all our emotions. We can then express what we need and connect through desire. You can see this illustrated in the case below.

Omar believes that Charlotte is responsible for the departure of several strong team members. Omar has never found the courage to tell Charlotte this. I sense tension in the room. We are guiding Omar to deliver this difficult message to Charlotte in an honest and connecting way. She is taken aback but shows understanding. She later feels grateful that several misunderstandings have been cleared up. The invisible conflict is replaced by shared commitments in their collaboration.

If you consult a handbook on positive psychology, you will find that working with strengths, experiencing emotions, and expressing them in communication contribute to connection. These practices were thoroughly addressed in this scenario. We hope that you also feel inspired to apply this in your practice.

'Connection is the energy
that exists between people
when they feel seen, heard,
and valued.'

BRENÉ BROWN

MINDSET 'HYGIENE'

Mindsets are the mental framework for our lives. They are a deeply rooted network of thoughts. Our mindset, like a camera lens, filters through its prism how we see the world. Our mindset colours what is possible. It also colours what is not possible. This determines our expectations, whether we are aware of it or not. What if we were to tidy up our thought patterns? What if we were open to a monthly or quarterly evaluation of our beliefs to see if and how they work for us? If they work, great. If not, we can choose to change them, to observe something else through a new lens. We can be more powerful than we realise, simply by analysing, understanding, and challenging what is in our heads. How powerful do we want to be?

A positive mindset is one of the patterns of corporate positivity. If you want to move towards a positive mindset with and within your organisation, the following four habits are essential:

1. Helping people feel valued.
2. Seeing solutions rather than problems.
3. Working in flow.
4. Seeking feedback and feedforward.

A FIRST HABIT: HELPING PEOPLE FEEL VALUED

We focus on the difference between recognition and appreciation to explore this habit. After that, we invite you to reflect on how powerful you are in expressing appreciation. When a colleague does something well, submits a report neatly on time, or manages the maintenance of the machinery effectively, we give recognition. 'Well done, thank you!' This is a reaction to what a colleague has done. Recognition is a reactive tool to compliment a colleague on their results. 'I greatly appreciate you. You truly make a difference' is a way to express your appreciation. The colleague feels they matter, regardless of the work they do. They are valued as a person, for who they are. It's not about performance. It's about the intrinsic value as a colleague and a person. Simply put: recognition is about what people do; appreciation is about who they are.

We often use the words 'recognition' and 'appreciation' interchangeably. However, as mentioned above, there is a significant difference between the two. Recognition involves giving positive feedback based on results or achievements. Appreciation, on the other hand, is about acknowledging someone's inherent value. This distinction is important. Recognition and appreciation are given for different reasons. Even when people succeed, there are inevitably challenges along the way. If we focus solely on applauding positive outcomes, on recognition, we miss many opportunities to connect with team members and support them, to appreciate them for who they are. For leaders who want their teams to thrive and for organisations that wish to create a positive culture, understanding this distinction is crucial. Paying attention to both recognition and appreciation requires a positive mindset.

Through this link, you will find some beautiful examples of how receiving appreciation is experienced.

This case clearly illustrates how a lack of appreciation for the coachee Oliver's moral sensitivity, his 'human uniqueness', impacts his well-being.

A HR director from a large company reaches out to us. He asks whether we can initiate a coaching programme for Oliver, his facility manager. Oliver is not feeling well at work. HR has had Oliver attend a couple of resilience training sessions. A confidant has also been appointed for him. Several discussions have already taken place. Nothing is working. Oliver loves his job, yet he simultaneously feels a sense of unhappiness in it. This paradox is baffling the HR director, who has yet to find an explanation. Oliver is valued for his expertise, and the organisation does not want to lose him.

After speaking with Oliver in a couple of sessions, he tells us that he indeed loves his job, is proud of his expertise, grateful to work with great colleagues, and convinced that he is employed by a good employer.

'What is going on here?' we wonder along with Oliver. Oliver does not feel appreciated. His sense of morality feels completely undermined. In his perception, there is no fairness in the organisation. Oliver strives for equal treatment for everyone in carrying out their job. No extra privileges for employee X, Y, or Z. No bigger car, no exceeding pay scales for those who shout louder. Oliver has substantial legal knowledge to safeguard this in a fair and rule-abiding manner.

The coaching programme helps Oliver gain insight into why he feels unwell: his moral sensitivity is being compromised. Now that he can articulate this, he feels empowered to have an open conversation with his manager to express himself as a 'person'. The conversation is not about technical matters but about Oliver as an individual. It has been agreed that he will write down his vision for an inclusive HR policy. Oliver is establishing the project team and values the personal development this brings him.

We each possess our own guidebook for feeling appreciated. Be ready to help your coworkers.

Care for Others as You Care for Yourself

Here I am. Have you noticed me? Have you seen what I need? Helping colleagues feel valued is not an empty notion. It requires effort. Appreciation demands skills. These can be developed. We can only appreciate when we listen strength-based, observe strength-based, communicate constructively, and approach others with wonder and curiosity.

Self-reflection on the skills of strength-based listening, strength-based observing, constructive communication, and being curious and in wonder about others brings insights. What is your answer to the following questions?

- *Do you mainly tell or ask?*
- *Do you also notice emotions in your colleagues, or only rationality?*
- *Are your conversations mainly task-oriented or connection-oriented?*
- *What is the balance between compliments/confirmation/recognition/appreciation and criticism/denial/doubt?*
- *Do you focus more on what your colleague means to you or on what they want to achieve?*
- *Are you aware of what you value in your colleague, independent of what they do?*
- *Do you pay attention to recognition and appreciation?*

The real power of appreciation lies in authenticity, individuality, and thoughtfulness. Appreciation contributes to well-being, mutual trust, and increased motivation. We go to work with more pleasure and perform better. This has a positive impact on colleagues. Research and literature indicate that a lack of appreciation is a major reason why people change jobs. When we discuss appreciation with our clients, we often discover that the distinction between recognition and appreciation is not well understood. In 'employee surveys' and 'exit interviews', recognition is often primarily questioned. Appreciation receives little attention. Lack of recognition and appreciation are significant reasons for dissatisfaction or departure. International research (Gallup, 2022) (Gallup is best known for its 'Clifton-Strengths assessment') reveals shocking results:

- 81% of the surveyed executives say that recognition is not an important strategic priority for the organisation.
- 73% of senior management say that their organisation does not offer training in 'best practices' for employee recognition.
- 76% of executives say they give recognition a few times a week, whereas only 40% of employees experience this.

We have not found any figures on appreciation…

A SECOND HABIT: SEEING SOLUTIONS RATHER THAN PROBLEMS

We guide you through several insights about perceiving problems. This will subsequently help you shift towards solutions. From there, we explain how this determines resilience. We conclude with some practical suggestions on how to work on this.

Obstacles Come from Within, not from Without

What is perception, really? Perception is how we see, understand, and give meaning to things. What we perceive can be a source of strength or a source of weakness. Learning to see and think in terms of solutions starts with our view of the 'problem'. Where one person sees a crisis, another sees an opportunity. Everyone encounters problems, and everyone can learn to perceive these problems differently.

We can consciously choose to stop seeing the obstacles we face at work solely as problems. Events influence our thoughts. Our thoughts determine our feelings. Our feelings translate into our behaviour. We can consciously influence this process. Our behaviour is the basis of the reactions we receive. This requires self-examination.

Katie Byron (Byron, 2016) conducted extensive work in the field of self-inquiry. She is the designer of the RET training: Rational Emotive Training. The fundamental premise of this training is that it is not the event or obstacle itself that determines our thinking, feeling, and behaviour. Rather, it is our interpretation of the event or obstacle that plays this role. Byron defined four simple questions that can help in examining your interpretations.

1. Is it true?
2. Can you absolutely know that it is true?
3. How do you react when you believe that thought?
4. Who would you be without that thought?

The application and result of these four questions are illustrated in the following case.

Emma leads a team of four people. She is head of the Customer Services department in a media company. As often happens, more complaints than messages of appreciation end up in the team's inbox. This affects the team members' mindset. More and more, they become convinced that customers have unrealistic expectations about the profitability of the services offered. The team is losing motivation. The positive spirit is disappearing. Since our RET training, Emma knows that feelings are always preceded by a thought. A thought that arises from what happens. She realizes that the team is being influenced by their thoughts and feelings. In turn, these affect the sometimes harsh language used in emails to customers. This, in turn, creates negative customer reactions. We guide the team with a positive peer review using Byron Katie's four questions. This leads the team to the following discoveries:

1. *'Is it true that there are more complaints?'*
   'Absolutely,' the team confirms.
   'Is it also true that customers' expectations are unrealistic?'
   'We believe so,' the team responds.
2. *'Can we be absolutely certain that the expectations are unrealistic?'*
   'That's how we see it; so, it's not an absolute truth,' the team admits.
3. *'How do we react to this?'*
   'It tends to translate into the tone of our responses to customers,' a team member admits.
4. *'Who would we be as a team without this thought?'*
   'A team that is more consciously mindful of customer-focused thinking and writing,' the team concedes.
   The thinking now shifts from focusing on the problem to seeking solutions.
   The team members choose to establish and commit to a language charter for themselves.

Most of our thoughts are not true. Think of a recent event that you found unpleasant. Test for yourself whether you can challenge and replace the thoughts that arose. We will provide a fictional example.

- *The event: Henry says he doesn't find my brainstorm creative.*
- *My thought: Henry isn't a facilitator; he could be less critical.*
- *My feeling: I feel a bit irritated.*
- *My behaviour: I ignore Henry.*
- *The consequence: During the lunch break, there's an unspoken tension that feels unpleasant between us.*

Write down your event, starting from self-examination. Look for a thought that might make you feel better and consequently lead to different behaviour.

- *The event: Henry says he doesn't find my brainstorm creative.*
- *My thought: Henry is open and has my best interests at heart. He wants to give me a tip that I can use in future sessions.*
- *My feeling: I feel a bit uncomfortable, but there is no resistance within me, rather gratitude.*
- *My behaviour: I thank Henry.*
- *The consequence: We continue to share our thoughts during the lunch break.*

We also find ourselves having these thoughts. Fortunately, we have the reflex to rely on Byron Katie's four questions to consciously influence our behaviour.

The problem is nothing more than the path to the solution

Each of us encounters obstacles, whether justified or not. The same rule applies in every context. The obstacle itself is not the most important thing. How we view it and how we respond to it determines how successful we are in overcoming it. We can turn a negative situation into an opportunity to discover chances and possibilities.

We often react rationally or emotionally, with emotion usually prevailing over reason when facing problems. Think of Emma's team in the earlier case, or Henry in the recent brainstorming session. Consider an impossible deadline being imposed: 'What are they thinking?' and 'What's the point of this?' are questions that might arise. This can cause us to lose perspective. In coaching interventions and positive peer reviews, we like to use Katie Byron's four questions to help the coachee or peer reviewer realise this. Only when we can objectively look at a problem can the next step be taken. Only then can we shift our focus to the opportunity that lies behind the problem. This requires courage, self-confidence, and resilience.

With what mindset do you greet problems?

Resilience Can Be Learned

We tend to see resilient people as those who accept setbacks with a smile and effortlessly laugh off their problems. This is not resilience. Resilience is the ability to bounce back, time and time again, from every obstacle we encounter. We can all demonstrate resilience. Admittedly, some people are more resilient than others, but it is not a trait you either have or don't have. Resilience can be learned and built. We often come across employees in organisations who are nearing the limits of their resilience. Under the pressure of change, targets, workload, tension among colleagues, and other challenges, they lose themselves. Such is the case with Ahmed in the following scenario.

The way Ahmed deals with adversity in this case is referred to as his coping style, specifically an active coping style. There are two ways to deal with setbacks: actively and passively. With an active coping style, like Ahmeds, you tackle the event almost immediately. In contrast, with a passive coping style, you create more distance and avoid the situation. Both approaches can reduce stress and tension in the short term. There is no one strategy that is always appropriate. The flexibility to switch between coping styles makes you resilient, allowing you to truly adapt to your context.

Utrecht University conducted research on coping styles and designed a list: the Utrecht Coping List. The list provides insight into how we deal with stressful events. Seven coping strategies are assessed, giving us an understanding of which strategies we might use more often or which others we could employ more frequently in different situations.

- Actively and immediately addressing the issue
- Attempting to 'numb' ourselves
- Avoiding or ignoring the problem
- Seeking comfort and support from others
- Reacting passively
- Expressing emotions
- Summoning reassuring thoughts

A mediocre evaluation at work upsets us. We wonder what's at stake: our job security, the respect of our colleagues, our own sense of competence. One way to deal with this is to ask the manager for advice on how to improve in the future. We channel our efforts in this direction. We might also look for another job. We might decide that the job isn't that important to us and choose to spend more time with our family and friends. We might decide to start each workday with five minutes of meditation. We might distract ourselves from the hassle at work with drugs and alcohol—not an effective long-term strategy, but perhaps we consider it a short-term one. Which coping style do you rely on the most?

We can work on our resilience. We don't need to wait until things go wrong. Everything starts with a healthy mind in a healthy body. Good fitness helps us to deal with both physical and mental challenges. The quality of our social relationships also impacts resilience. Moreover, we become more resilient when we expand our skills and make use of our talents and qualities. Positive character traits also strengthen resilience.

Enhancing Resilience

Just as in nature, it is flexibility and adaptability that contribute most to human survival. Al Siebert (Siebert, 2005), an American psychologist known for his research on psychological resilience, describes five simple steps to cultivate greater resilience. By consciously engaging with these five levels, you can increase your resilience. The more you apply them, the more resilience you will cultivate.

- Take care of your physical and mental health. Regularly ask yourself: 'How do I feel about what's happening?' 'What am I doing to take care of myself?'

- Look outward: Develop skills for solving difficulties such as analytical thinking, creativity, and empathetic listening. When you recognise problems, take the time to think and investigate what the underlying causes might be. Can you control them? If so, what strategies and plans will you make to solve the problems? If not, how can you adjust your actions and behaviour so that things turn out well?

- Also look inward: Develop a positive self-image and self-confidence. Do not waste too much energy on things you cannot control and do not dwell on the past for too long. Stay engaged, be productive, and strive for positive outcomes. Value and respect yourself, regardless of whether you are good at something. Good self-esteem is the foundation for a healthy dose of self-confidence.

- Adopt a positive attitude and look around: Develop your curiosity. Ask questions and enjoy learning. Look for solutions that are good for yourself and for others.

- Find the positive in setbacks: Turn misfortune into fortune. According to Siebert, this is the highest level of resilience. 'What have I learned?', 'What can I be grateful for?', 'What new quality have I discovered about myself?'

Mindset is the only sustainable way to move from complaint to strength.

A THIRD HABIT: WORKING IN FLOW

Flow is an essential concept when discussing a positive mindset. We explain flow, examine flow triggers and inhibitors, and provide an illuminating case study.

Mihaly Csikszentmihalyi is best known for his work on flow, a state of complete engagement and focus on an activity. His work has influenced research and practice regarding flow in various fields such as psychology, education, sports, and business. Flow is a state of consciousness where an individual is fully immersed in an activity, feeling involved and focused. This can occur in any context: preparing a presentation, performing a complex task, writing a book. We have also witnessed this ⌣.

Csikszentmihalyi suggests that achieving flow can lead to feelings of happiness, enjoyment, and fulfilment (Csikszentmihalyi, 1990). Anyone can enter a state of flow. In flow, concentration becomes so intensely focused that everything else falls away. Action and awareness merge. Our sense of self and self-consciousness completely disappear. Time vanishes, it slows down or speeds up. We let go of our beliefs. The English poet John Milton was blind. Thomas Edison was deaf when he invented the phonograph. Ludwig Beethoven was profoundly deaf when he composed the Ninth Symphony. He never heard it, except in his mind. Despite the limitations these famous individuals had, they succeeded in creating something great in flow. Flow allows us to do things we might have thought were beyond the limits of our abilities.

Flow is a paradoxical combination of:
- Self-confidence and total surrender;
- Relaxation and concentration;
- Inner calm and immense alertness;
- Complete control and total letting go;
- Strength and flexibility.

It is a mental state so complete that we become entirely absorbed in what we are doing. In this state, we can perform exceptionally well.

Doing as Many Things as Possible to Achieve Flow

When we experience moments of flow, we feel happier than when we rarely or never experience flow. This is the key conclusion from numerous studies, regardless of the age, education, or background of the respondents. Choosing activities that lead to the creation of flow brings order to our minds. A clear action plan helps. There is a focus on the goal, and energy is invested in a task. Structure emerges in our thoughts and actions. Consider, for example, preparing a keynote presentation. You think about what you want to achieve, the story you want to tell, how you will approach it, and what knowledge and skills you will use. You also create a stimulating context: a clean desk, coffee, music, and so on. This helps us build psychological capital through flow. According to Csikszentmihalyi, this happens when we develop our skills to tackle higher levels of challenges.

Figure 8 clarifies the conditions necessary to achieve flow: a good balance between challenges and skills, and a good balance between boredom and stress or anxiety. A good balance between challenges and skills involves taking on tasks that push the boundaries of your knowledge and abilities but deciding to tackle them anyway. A good balance between boredom and stress or anxiety involves taking on assignments that are outside your usual routine, thereby slightly unsettling you.

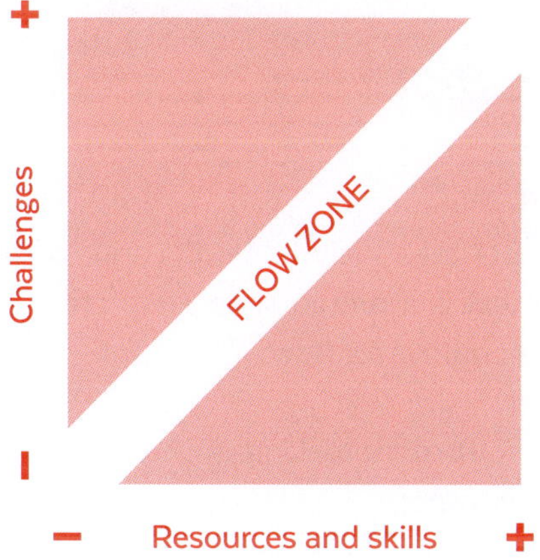

Figure 8. How to Reach the Flow Zone?

'The Psychology of Optimal Experience'

In 1990, Csikszentmihalyi's work came to the forefront in government, business, and the arts. The concepts have since been translated into dozens of languages and are used by diverse organisations such as Cirque du Soleil and Montessori schools, the British Cabinet and the Getty Museum. Nissan applied flow to car design to make driving more enjoyable. Newsweek magazine wrote that Flow was one of President Clinton's favourite books. The Austrian Cabinet invited Csikszentmihalyi to speak to them about how flow could influence education in the twenty-first century.

Flow Blockers and Flow Inducers

Flow does not occur spontaneously. It is not a spur-of-the-moment inspiration. Creating a context is a prerequisite. Here are some more practical examples of creating a context for flow:

- Stop multitasking: start monotasking.
- Set clear goals and sub-goals.
- Ensure mental peace: avoid being overwhelmed with too many thoughts.
- Avoid distractions such as emails, calls, chat windows, pop-ups, and unnecessary documents.

- Put on some music: it enhances concentration. Spotify has good play-lists.
- Write down to-do lists and keep them out of sight.
- Allocate time for tasks that require concentration: don't schedule time when you have a meeting an hour later.
- Make sure you have something to drink and eat: you stay in flow longer when not interrupted by hunger or thirst.
- Develop a stimulating balance between challenge and skill: constantly raise the bar. The challenge should always demand a bit extra from you.
- Consciously consider the qualities that will help you.
- Take slow breaths now and then: it slows your brain waves.

We all have flow enhancers and are challenged by our flow inhibitors.

Flow inducers ensure that:
- *You clearly know what you are working towards*
- *You are doing something you enjoy*
- *You are fully committed to the task*
- *You have confidence in yourself and your abilities*
- *You receive feedback and feedforward on it*

These are clear flow inhibitors:
- *A lack of self-confidence*
- *Prejudices about the task you are undertaking*
- *A lack of discipline*
- *Indecisiveness*
- *Self-criticism*
- *Fear, stress, or insufficient mental rest*

When we work on achieving flow, we often do this through a physical setup in a three-step movement: we describe the flow inhibitor, counteract it with a positive counterpart, and determine a concrete action. This was also our approach with Roberto in the following case.

During a workshop, Roberto indicates that he is struggling to concentrate on preparing for a corrective feedback conversation. He doubts whether it is appropriate to have the conversation at all. This doubt takes over and prevents him from taking action. This thought is a flow inhibitor. He feels restless in his mind. We put three placemats on the ground. The first describes the flow inhibitor, the second the thought of a positive counterpart, and the third the concrete action. Roberto stands on the first placemat and loudly expresses his thought about the feedback conversation: 'Am I the right person to have this conversation?' We get Roberto moving by asking him which thought would help him achieve a state of flow to prepare himself.

Roberto describes the positive counterpart as follows: 'Whatever I bring up in the feedback conversation, I do it with the best intentions.' The concrete action he will undertake is to deepen his skill in connected communication. He takes action and books an appointment in his diary. We take note and agree to follow up on his experience. He has managed to leave the worrying behind. The flow inhibitor has disappeared. It spurred him into action. The deepening in connected communication brought him joy. The feedback conversation itself will take place later.

Flow is not 'going with the flow' where we let ourselves be carried away by the current.

A FOURTH HABIT: SEEKING FEEDBACK AND FEEDFORWARD

As experts, we are often asked to integrate working towards a continuous feedback culture into our projects. Books, the press, and social media are full of it. Feedback his high on everyone's agenda, receiving significant emphasis and attention, yet it remains a challenge to embed it into the culture. A feedforward culture is even less discussed. In this chapter, we highlight the following: fear of rejection and desire for social acceptance; triggers when receiving feedback; growth through feedforward; a growth mindset that loves feedback and feedforward.

During a recent study, 62 coworkers at a large consultancy firm were brought into a room in pairs. They did not know each other. They were asked to perform a role play. Researchers asked them to sit opposite each other, not as colleagues but as 'adversaries'. They were to negotiate the purchase and sale of a company. They had six minutes to negotiate the price. Heart rate monitors tracked the ups and downs of their heart rates during the negotiation. After the negotiations, each party provided feedback on the other's performance during the role play. Some participants were instructed to give feedback unsolicited. Others were instructed to ask for feedback. The heart rate monitors silently listened.

This is what the researchers found. If you want to put people on edge, tell them they will receive feedback. Or, just as well, tell them they will be giving feedback. The subjects in the study felt equally anxious about giving and receiving feedback.

Social Acceptance and Rejection

The primary reason why embedding feedback into the organisational culture remains challenging is the fear of social rejection. People have a fundamental need for positive and enduring relationships, for social acceptance. Deep down, even the most hardened criminal yearns for the same as an innocent baby: love and social acceptance. Social acceptance is pleasant, provides recognition, brings appreciation, and is associated with various indicators of well-being. Recently, much attention has been given in the social-psychological literature to the flip side of social acceptance, namely social rejection. The human need for social connectedness can thus be both a sweet blessing when others accept us, and a bitter curse when others reject us.

People experience social acceptance and rejection in countless ways. Examples of acceptance include being hired for an exciting job, receiving a promotion at work, being asked to participate in a strategic project, and receiving positive feedback. Examples of rejection include being dismissed, being ignored by colleagues, not being invited to a meeting, bullying, inappropriate behaviour, and so forth.

Corrective feedback is not social rejection. There is a positive intention behind corrective feedback: facilitating a change or addition to help the other person in their development. Nevertheless, we sometimes perceive it as social rejection. Our brains are biologically programmed to flee from corrective feedback. Research shows that we unconsciously protect ourselves (by fighting, fleeing, or freezing) because we feel threatened. Our brains automatically code 'negative' feedback as a threat to our social acceptance and identity. Biologically, it is thus difficult for our primal instinct to open up when corrective feedback comes our way.

The Three Triggers When Receiving Feedback

There is much emphasis on giving feedback at work, but perhaps the most underrated skill is receiving it. We are often inclined to take a defensive stance. We feel affected in some way. We disagree with the message; we doubt the other person and did not expect this feedback; we perceive it as a personal attack. This causes discomfort. It triggers something within us (Stone & Heen, 2015). We would like to discuss actively seeking out and receiving feedback with an open mindset with you.

Does consciously seeking feedback not always appear prominently on your radar too? That subconscious fear of what you might receive may be playing a part. We invite you to take a stroll through your recent memory and look for moments when you received corrective feedback that stuck with you. The more, the better. Compare them to what follows. Which triggers affected you?

- *Truth Triggers: 'The challenge to see'*
  We disagree with the content of the feedback. We find it incorrect, unfair, incomplete, exaggerated, etc. 'That's wrong. That's not helpful. I'm very sceptical about that.'

- *Relationship Triggers: 'The challenge of we'*
  Something about the feedback giver triggers us. We find the person unreliable or not credible. We question their motives. 'After all I've done for you. Who are you to say that? You're the problem, not me.'

- *Identity Triggers: 'The challenge of me'*
  Our story about who we are is under attack. Our alarm bells ring, and the brain switches to its defence mechanism. 'I mess up everything. I'm not a bad person. That's not who I am.'

When you return to the walk through your brain just now, looking for moments when you received corrective feedback that stuck, do you recognise yourself in any of these triggers?

Feedforward Retrieval

From the perspective of positive psychology, it has long been advocated that it is more effective to focus on what we do want rather than on what we do not want. Feedforward is part of a positive mindset. With feedforward, we look to the future. We explore achievable options that make us feel good and commit to action. In feedforward, we direct the insights we seek. This stimulates positive thinking and creates new opportunities. We directly ask others for information about our own functioning with the intention of further growth in the future. We show our vulnerability and thereby also create trust with others.

If we want to take control of our own actions, personal growth, and development, it is beneficial to regularly engage the people around us in our growth. Simply by asking questions. By being vulnerable and asking people from all corners of our environment, 360 degrees, 'How do you think I am doing? Do you have any tips for me?' By asking for feedforward, we focus on the future. This makes the 'harvest' much easier for our brains to process. By having control over the questions we ask, we put our brains in a learning mode rather than a defensive mode.

Growth Mindset

The American psychologist Carol Dweck, affiliated with Stanford University, has spent decades researching why some people are successful in life and continue to develop, while others, equally talented, remain stagnant. She discovered that the mindset of individuals plays a crucial role in their learning process.

Carol Dweck (Dweck, 2006) identified two types of mindsets: the fixed mindset and the growth mindset. A mindset is a way of thinking that determines how you view yourself, your qualities, and abilities. A growth-oriented mindset assumes that you can develop your intelligence, qualities, and skills. Someone with a growth-oriented mindset is committed to practice and perseveres in the face of setbacks. They are also open to feedback, viewing it as a learning opportunity. When others succeed, it is seen as a moment for learning and inspiration. Conversely, someone with a fixed mindset believes that intelligence, qualities, and skills are innate and unchangeable, making practice seem pointless. Individuals with a fixed mindset are also afraid of appearing foolish, making mistakes, and taking risks. Feedback is often ignored and interpreted as criticism and a threat.

The work of Carol Dweck demonstrates that these two mindsets have a significant impact on people's ability to learn and develop. Individuals who utilise their growth mindset can achieve more and grow further. They can also do so in less time than those with a fixed mindset. Specifically, a fixed mindset, when learning a new skill, says things like: 'I'm not good at this', 'I give up, this is too hard', 'This is going to take too long', 'I've already made two mistakes', 'Plan A didn't work', and so forth. Conversely, the growth mindset tends to say: 'What can I do to improve?', 'I'll try one of the strategies we learned', 'This takes time and effort, but I'll do it', 'What can I learn from my mistakes?', 'Plan A didn't work, but luckily the alphabet has 26 letters.'

- *Acknowledge and embrace your shortcomings.*
  - *If you hide from your weaknesses, you will never overcome them.*
- *See challenges as opportunities.*
  - *Having a growth mindset means daring to enjoy the opportunities you receive and allowing yourself to improve.*
- *Try different learning methods.*
  - *There is no single model for learning. What works for one person may not work for another and vice versa.*
- *Replace the word 'failure' with the word 'learning.'*
  - *If you make a mistake or miss a goal, you haven't failed; you have learned.*
- *Stop seeking approval.*
  - *Prioritising approval over learning will come at the expense of your growth potential.*
- *Value the process over the end result.*
  - *Learn to enjoy the process of learning itself, regardless of the goal to be achieved, even if it sometimes progresses slower than you'd like.*
- *Emphasise growth over speed.*
  - *Learning quickly is not the same as learning well, and good learning sometimes requires time to make mistakes.*

* *Be proud of your process.*
- *Focus on your learning process and the efforts you've made. Compliment yourself and celebrate successes.*

And above all, become aware of the mindset with which you start your development.

Beliefs Influence Our Brain Activity

Research indicates that there is a connection between our beliefs and our brain activity. When people with a growth mindset make a mistake, more brain activity is measured compared to those with a fixed mindset. The brains of individuals who believed in their ability to improve reacted differently when a mistake was made than the brains of those who did not. The study also found that individuals with a growth mindset were more aware of their mistakes than those with a fixed mindset. They are more likely to go back and correct their errors.

The relationship between our beliefs and the functioning of our brains is clear. If you believe in yourself, and do not think that your ability is fixed, your brain shows more activity and grows when mistakes are made. The fact that brain activity is greatest when people have a growth mindset demonstrates how important it is for individuals to believe in themselves and understand that brains can grow and change through hard work.

Source: Mangels et al. 2006

The field of positive psychology has brought a wealth of insights into understanding what contributes to a positive mindset. Mindset is crucial for fostering a positive organisational culture. Our thinking influences our feelings, desires, and actions. In this context, the following topics emerged in this pattern: expressing appreciation; solution-focused thinking; working in flow; seeking feedback and feedforward; adopting a growth mindset.

'PEOPLE WILL FORGET WHAT YOU SAID, PEOPLE WILL FORGET WHAT YOU DID, BUT PEOPLE WILL NEVER FORGET HOW YOU MADE THEM FEEL.'

MAYA ANGELOU

COMMUNICATION

YOU GET WHAT YOU GIVE

Maya Angelou's quote captures the essence of positive communication for us. Communication creates. It creates experiences and builds relationships. If we remove communication, we also remove relationships. When you communicate, you work on relationships. You relate. Each of us has the potential to become a great communicator and to connect deeply with others. Positive communication not only leaves an impression on the listener but also offers health and well-being benefits for the speaker.

Positive communication is one of the patterns of corporate positivity. If you wish to move towards positive communication within and for your organisation, the following four habits are essential:

1. Inspiring around the vision and objectives.
2. Consciously using positive statements.
3. Giving room to opinions and interaction.
4. Conveying hope and optimism.

A FIRST HABIT: INSPIRING AROUND THE VISION AND OBJECTIVES

The primary role of vision and objectives in organisations is to focus on human energy. It should be an exciting narrative that makes everyone eager to contribute. The future is clearly defined for all. The journey to create clarity about a vision starts with reflecting on the past, experiencing the present, and providing a perspective for the future. Passion, what lies closest to the heart, drives the development of a vision. It is a dynamic process that adapts to changing circumstances and new insights. Only shared visions possess the magnetic power to stimulate and maintain engagement. Both a small department of ten and an organisation of a hundred or a thousand people require a meaningful vision. Communicating about it inspiringly ensures sustainability. But how do you do that? In this chapter, we look at the 'golden circle' as a tool for inspiring with the mission and vision. It unleashes human energy. We also discuss storytelling as a method to communicate positively.

Clarity of Mission and Vision

When we browse through the websites of various organisations, we notice that there are many and varied interpretations of mission and vision. During interactions with clients, we consistently inquire about their mission and vision. Even then, the answers are not always clear-cut. If we want to shift the culture of organisations towards a dynamic entity, a coherent story is necessary. For this, we use the well-known, concrete, and pragmatic approach of Simon Sinek (2009). We still find it a relevant foundation, strong in its simplicity.

Simon Sinek's Golden Circle

The concept of the 'golden circle' is inspired by a simple mathematical ratio that has fascinated mathematicians, biologists, architects, artists, musicians, and naturalists for centuries. It supports the idea that there is more order in nature than we might think. For instance, consider the symmetry of leaves or the perfection of snowflakes. Just as in nature, the golden circle provides predictability in human behaviour. The golden circle helps us understand why we do what we do. It explains why people get the Harley-Davidson logo tattooed on their bodies. It clarifies why people embrace Patagonia.

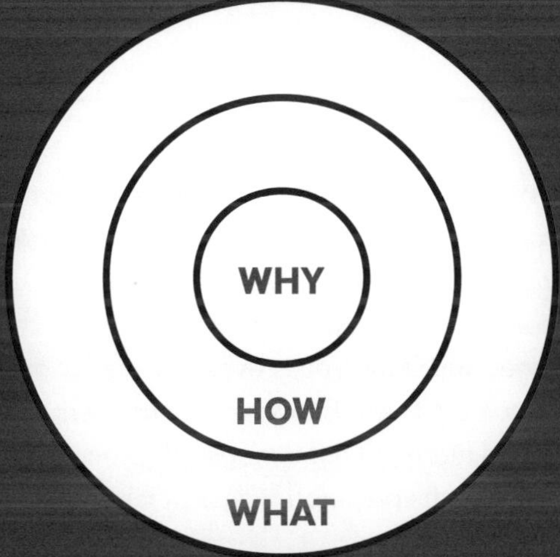

Figure 9. Simon Sinek's Golden Circle.

The Golden Circle starts from the inside out. It consists of a structure of three circles: a clear Why, a disciplined How, and a consistent What. Everything the organisation says and does endorses the Why, the mission. The Why is a belief, a conviction. The How, the vision, describes how to realise the Why. Strengths, values, and norms are the guiding principles. The What includes the products, services, and tasks.

Patagonia's mission is as follows: "Patagonia is in business to save our home planet." Their vision is: "We aspire to be a company where people from all backgrounds, identities and experiences have the power to con-

When the mission and vision are clear, we can make hundreds of micro-decisions. It works like a compass that is constantly referred to. The goals are aligned with it. This makes it clear why objectives are formulated. This process happens step by step, as illustrated in the case below.

We meet a client who is looking for a way to create connection within a new account management team. Apart from their names and previous roles, the team members do not know each other. During our first meeting with the team, the focus quickly shifts to aligning the CRM system, distributing clients, and setting objectives. The idea of organising a client event is also discussed. Overall, it was a productive meeting. However, a sense of unity as a team did not emerge. We propose scheduling a follow-up meeting, with the preparation task of reflecting on why the team exists in the first place.

During the second meeting, we gather the thoughts of the team members. Each person has their own opinion on the team's purpose. Through debate, opinions, and interactions, we succeed in formulating the purpose. The "why" is clear. Everyone is passionate. This is the reason we get up in the morning to work. The connection that has formed among the team members is strongly felt. The vision will be clarified in a subsequent brainstorming session. It is decided to communicate the vision clearly to the other departments. The communication department is involved to provide a professional perspective. Some team members arrange meetings with leaders of other departments to present their team. Our task is complete. Today, two years later, posts about the team's vision and how they realise it daily still appear on LinkedIn.

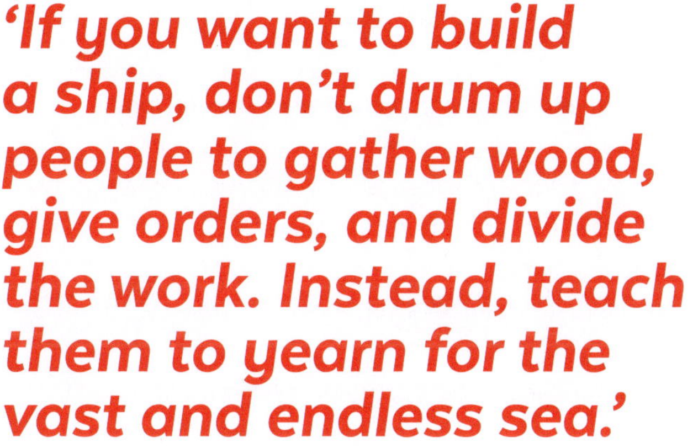

'If you want to build a ship, don't drum up people to gather wood, give orders, and divide the work. Instead, teach them to yearn for the vast and endless sea.'

ANTOINE DE SAINT-EXUPÉRY

Stories Set Things in Motion

How do we move from an idea to action? From the first step to the next? How do we take these steps together? How do we get moving again after being stuck? How do we inspire with a vision and goals to lead everyone into the future? Imagination is sometimes viewed with suspicion in organisations. Does it belong there? Should we not stick to reality with numbers and facts? Organisations do not like castles in the air, but they also cannot rely solely on well-founded strategic documents. Our imagination is crucial for envisioning new possibilities. This is why we speak of the power of imagination. How can we positively use the 'magic' of stories to enable development and movement?

Storytelling, a Way to Communicate Positively

Everyone can tell stories. Translating a vision into a story inspires. It encourages people to leave familiar paths and embark on new journeys. Through storytelling, we bring imaginative tales to people, bringing information to life. This creates an emotional bond between the person and the story, making it memorable and understandable. Storytelling is one of the oldest methods of conveying a message. Remarkable figures from history, strong brands, and notable organisations all have a story attached to them.

This is all due to the way our brain works: stories make abstract concepts concrete, place people at the centre, and deal with emotions. Stories engage the head, heart, and hands. The head envisions the future and provides direction. The heart inspires and engages. The hands execute and innovate. Start the story by naming the desire, do not shy away from sharing the obstacles, be open to the wildest fantasies that have arisen, and give language to how movement has emerged.

Our brain is inspired by stories and remembers through the meaning of the story, the coherence, emotion, and social connection. Stories stimulate action and produce chemicals that make us feel good. Figure 10 illustrates what stories do: connect; understand; remember; touch; prompt action and create a good feeling and reward.

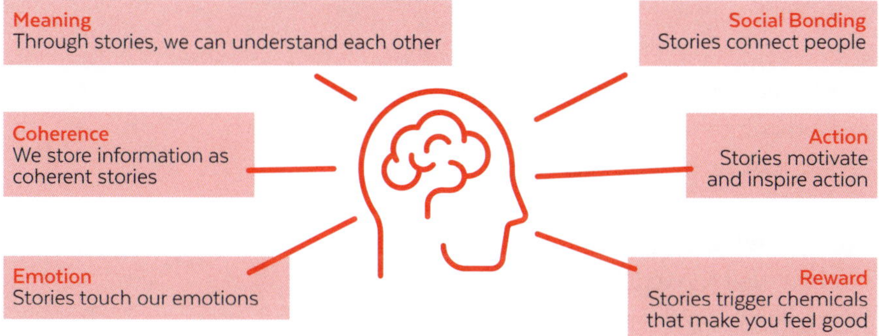

Figure 10. Our Brain and Stories.

Storytelling means sharing something in a connecting way and serving each other mutually. Communication that sidelines the heart can never be true communication. Such a substitute is not aimed at sharing and inspiring but at convincing, being right and getting something from the other. Inspire with the vision and objectives from who you want to be. Tell your story and make sure it is safeguarded within the organisation.

A SECOND HABIT: CONSCIOUSLY USING POSITIVE STATEMENTS

When we use language that indicates we are losing courage, hope and the chance of finding a solution become particularly small. Consider statements like: 'I have worked several weekends on this report. The end result is not good. What to do next is a mystery to me.' We remain stuck in a problem by thinking and talking about it in a problem-focused way. This does not help us or others move forward. We often find in organisations that 'problem talking' is part of the culture. Corporate positivity pushes people towards solution-oriented language. In this chapter, we are excited to share the impact of positive language use. We discuss how you can empower others' messages. We end with the importance of language use in achieving goals.

Positive Language Towards Solutions

In all openness, what do you say spontaneously?
It is difficult to find a suitable answer.
We are looking for a suitable answer.

Admit it. What do you think?
I have to do this well.
I am going to do this well.

Dare to show your true colours. How do you address the other person?
Can I disturb you for five minutes?
Do you have a moment for me?

Honestly, which side are you most often on?
I can't do this.
I can't do this yet.

How can you use solution-oriented language so that positive statements become audible and tangible? We provide a few tips:

- Use past tense when talking about problems rather than present or future tense. 'I was tense' instead of 'I am tense'.
- Talk about what you do want instead of what you don't want. 'I want to make our customer curious about our product' instead of 'I want to convince our customers that we are better than the competition'.
- Avoid using 'all-or-nothing words' like always, never, nobody, everybody. They reduce the chances of hope and creative thinking. Use preferably usually, some, a few.
- Do not talk about yourself or others as the problem. This labels you and others negatively. 'He is a procrastinator' becomes 'He needs a bit more time'.
- Use language that conveys positive expectations. 'So far, I haven't found the right job' instead of 'It will be difficult to find a job that suits me'.
- Choose 'want to' instead of 'have to'. 'I want to do this well', not 'I have to do this well'.

- Go for 'doing' rather than 'trying'. Trying lacks determination. Doing is action.
- Replace 'why' with 'how'. 'Why' reinforces problem-focused thinking. 'How' provides energy to seek solutions.
- Resolve to 'find' instead of 'search'. 'I will find an answer', not 'I will search for an answer'. Finding reinforces a mindset to solve a problem.

We observed a pattern regarding language use during a meeting with one of our clients.

Communicating positively means paying attention to communication that energises, cares for the person, and achieves the desired result. Positive communication is therefore more than just using positive words. There are several gateways to enhance positive statements: adding dynamism to our statements through active language; adopting a solution-oriented attitude; paying attention to the feelings, needs, and qualities of our conversation partner.

Actively Constructive Responses to Positive Stories

Sharing positive experiences with colleagues has a beneficial impact on your well-being and that of your colleagues. This effect increases with the number of people with whom the experience is shared. In positive psychology, this is called 'capitalisation,' a snowball effect. There are four ways to respond to good news, such as your colleague's promotion (Gable, 2004).

- **Actively and Constructively**
  "That's fantastic. I know you've worked hard for this. You more than deserve this promotion. I'm curious and want to know all about it. When did you hear the news? What did your boss say? How did your family react?"
- **Passively and Constructively**
  "That's good news for you. Congratulations."
- **Passively and Destructively**
  "Glad to hear it. What do you think? Shall we go for lunch together?"
- **Actively and Destructively**
  "Your manager made a good decision. But are you ready for it? You're going to need to work hard to get up to speed. This will cost you your free time. Be aware that there won't be any space for it during work hours."

Do you recognise these patterns? Do you intervene when necessary? It's in our best interest to use actively constructive language. Responding actively and constructively is a form of positive communication. It is a valuable tool for deepening relationships and smoothing interactions. This is important for every manager, employee, in short, everyone who works with people (Gable, 2004).

Be a Rainbow in Someone Else's Cloud

By using positive statements, we care for others. We promote well-being. Words are powerful. They have the ability to affect our mood immediately and even linger in our thoughts and hearts forever. Philosopher Louis Castellanos is a pioneer in the study of positive language. He investigates how the brain's synaptic connections behave when using positive and negative words. He substantiates the power of words. Words can have an immediate effect on our mood. They can make or break. They linger, whether positive or negative. They are indelible from our memory. How can you promote well-being through language? The answer lies in the use of words. Positive language is more than just nice words. Positive language is the ability to tell our own story with different words. Language inhabits us 24 hours a day. Being consciously mindful of our language ensures that we express well-being to ourselves and others.

Achieving Goals with Positive Language

We follow Kim Cameron in his assertion that achieving goals in an organisation is linked to the positive language that prevails in its culture. The mere use of the word 'no' is enough to release the stress hormone cortisol in the brain. To be successful, adapting our language is essential. We create perspective and involve others in possibilities. People who make positive statements give energy to others. This ensures that others enjoy being around them. This creates group dynamics. A dynamic of wanting to achieve and believing it is possible. The link with mindset is clear. Let us look together at the language that enables us, as Kim Cameron says, to achieve 'Mount Everest goals'.

- **Don't** - What went wrong?
  Do - What went well, even if just a little bit?
- **Don't** - What is the problem?
  Do - How is that a problem for you, for your team?
- **Don't** - How did the problem arise?
  Do - What or who can help solve the problem?
- **Don't** - When does the problem occur and what are the consequences?
  Do - When were there exceptions to the problem and what were the consequences?
- **Don't** - What do you want to get rid of?
  Do - What do you want to achieve?
- **Don't** - How did you get into this situation?
  Do - How can you get out of it?
- **Don't** - What do you find difficult about it?
  Do - What do you see as a challenge in it?
- **Don't** - What do you want to learn?
  Do - What do you want to get better at?

A THIRD HABIT: GIVING ROOM TO OPINIONS AND INTERACTION

Opinions are views that people hold about certain topics. These views can be based on information, personal experiences, beliefs, values, facts, or emotions. Opinions can range from positive to negative. They significantly influence how people in organisations think, feel, and act. They determine how people handle changes and challenges at work. Guiding the formation of opinions contributes to a positive work environment and aids in making effective decisions.

A socially safe and positive organisation is an environment where we are allowed to show ourselves: our intentions, ideas, emotions, doubts, questions, needs, and problems. We are allowed to form an opinion and share it with others. Interactions refer to the way people communicate and engage with one another. Opinions can either stimulate or restrict interactions. An organisational culture develops where people collaborate through interactions, actions, and reactions. How do you create an organisational culture that allows room for opinions and interaction? Focus on the quality of analytical thinking; employ 'liberating structures'; use Socratic questioning with conversation partners.

Opinion Formation and Analytical Thinking

A strong quality in opinion formation that often goes unnoticed is analytical thinking. People with analytical thinking gather information, analyse, and reason logically before forming an opinion. This quality makes a valuable contribution to opinion and decision-making, ensuring a balance between emotion and reason in often emotionally charged discussions.

- Identify individuals in your organisation who possess analytical thinking skills. Encourage them to participate in debates or group discussions. Analytical thinkers carefully consider what is being said before responding, which can help find common ground.
- Involve these individuals in data analysis.
- Encourage them to share their thought processes with others.

- Provide opportunities for them to share their views through written communication. This allows them to present their opinions in a structured way, enabling others to understand and respond to their reasoning.
- Ensure a safe environment for interactions to take place.

Challenging Opinions through Interactions

Every interaction is an opportunity to involve people in the vision and objectives. Aiming for positive movement is a group process that dynamically develops through continuous interaction. We can engage in debate based on opinions. Interactions invite others to respond or to see or do things differently. Robert E. Quinn, professor of management and organization (Quinn, 2015), refers to authentic conversations, where people can be themselves, as the key to positive organisations. Being yourself allows you to open up more easily to other people and ideas. According to research by Losada and Heaphy, higher-performing companies ask as many questions as they make statements. Companies that perform poorly, on average, ask five questions for every hundred statements (Losada & Heaphy, 2004).

'Liberating Structures'

Henri Lipmanowicz and Keith McCandless (Lipmanowicz & McCandless, 2021) developed a set of simple and powerful methods to help people collaborate more effectively, solve problems, and generate ideas. These methods, which they call 'liberating structures,' introduce small shifts in the way people interact with each other. Conventional structures are either too static, involving presentations, guided discussions, reports, etc., or too loose and disorganised, involving open discussions and brainstorming. They provide insufficient space for good ideas to emerge. Liberating structures give coworkers more ownership and responsibility in forming opinions and enable valuable interactions. They make it possible to build an organisation where everyone enjoys working. They can be used to engage everyone in, for example, transforming a vision into reality. Any coworker interested in contributing to the organisation of today and tomorrow can make use of 32 simple liberating structures. Curious? You can find all the Liberating Structures and the associated methods via this QR code.

Liberating structures harness collective intelligence, which comprises three layers: what we already know we know, what we don't yet know we know, and what we don't know yet but can develop together. Liberating structures stimulate energy and creativity by minimally structuring the way we interact with each other while leaving the content or subject matter open. Here are some we like to use in our interventions:

- 1-2-4-All: In '1-2-4-All', you engage each individual in the search for answers within a safe space for expression, without hierarchy. Silent conversations and diverse input are encouraged. The idea is to build from individual reflection to group reflection (1-2-4, etc.), until the main points are discussed collectively. You choose a topic, self-reflect, discuss in pairs, then in groups of four, and finally in a plenary session. This fosters consensus or shared understanding.

- Impromptu Networking: 'Impromptu Networking' helps to tap into curiosity and talent. It helps the team to focus collectively on a subject. Five elements for this method are determined in advance: purpose, principles, participants, structure, and practice. Around the defined subject, everyone shares something about themselves that they consider relevant. Each individual contribution is acknowledged, and the power of new connections between people and ideas is emphasised.

- Appreciative Inquiry: In 'Appreciative Inquiry', you build on successes that are shared. You consciously give time, space, and attention to the other person for that spontaneous moment. This also provides insights into what helps achieve extraordinary performances. New ways to reach those performances become visible in the organisation. This positive movement is fuelled by the search for what currently works and by uncovering the underlying reasons that make success possible.

Asking Questions Takes Practice

A question is often more than just a sentence with a question mark at the end. There is also what we call a genuine thinking question: you can only answer it by thinking about it. The Greek philosopher Socrates was one of the founders of methodical and simultaneously critical questioning. His perhaps most famous statement is: 'I only know that I know nothing.' Socrates primarily wanted to teach people to think critically. He believed that by acquiring (self-)knowledge, people became better individuals. The following case illustrates the power of a Socratic core question. It helps us to stay curious and avoid a defensive 'armoured' attitude.

In the context of a coaching assignment, we are asked to attend an investigative conversation between Amir, the sales director, and Janet, the sales team manager. Amir observes that his relationship with Janet is difficult, despite her good results, ambition, and dedication. She has met and exceeded her team targets for several consecutive quarters. Janet is very ambitious, which aligns perfectly with the organisation's growth strategy. The 'Employee Engagement Survey' confirms Amir's suspicions about Janet's management style. The feedback from the team indicates that Janet is indeed very results-oriented, but she micro-manages due to her desire to have the best figures in her region. The team says she manages in a top-down manner, without any flexibility in her approach. This dynamic is also present in the relationship between Amir and Janet: there is little room for discussion, and she always aims to prove her point.

During the conversation, we as coaches observe this pattern. Janet finds it hard to allow pauses and silences in the conversation. She seems to be 'armoured'. She also has a visible need to extensively defend her viewpoint. She equates the organisation's growth directly with numerical growth. We notice a similar pattern in Amir's responses to Janet. The conversation turns into a cat-and-mouse game. We pause the discussion, highlight the tension with some examples from the conversation, and ask both for approval to restart the conversation based on four princi-

A Socratic dialogue is a conversation in which we explore what we think and why. This approach involves postponing our judgement and truly listening to one another. We uncover different perspectives without getting bogged down in merely exchanging and often defending viewpoints and opinions. We can deepen the conversation and collectively arrive at wisdom. In an inquisitive dialogue, we question the other person and are ourselves critically questioned on what we say and how we substantiate our statements. A Socratic dialogue always centres around a thinking question. Therefore, the conversation does not begin with just any question, but with a targeted question that frames a relevant issue to gain new insights.

An example of a Socratic question is 'How should we conduct meetings?' A Socratic dialogue starts from a concrete, real-life experience of one of the participants with a certain issue. For instance: 'I notice that laptops are being used during team meetings and find this rather inappropriate.' This is then examined: 'Is it inappropriate to have laptops open during a team meeting?' Why or why not? In the ensuing conversation, participants experience how their thinking evolves: new nuances, arguments from others, questioning one's own views, doubting one's own perspectives, even to the point of completely changing viewpoints. By engaging in a Socratic dialogue, we no longer take our own thinking for granted.

In her bestseller Socrates on Sneakers, Elke Wiss provides numerous tips to become more proficient in Socratic questioning. Here are a few of them.

- *Be mindful of common pitfalls: ask questions instead of focusing too much on yourself; do not avoid questions out of fear of discomfort for yourself or others.*
- *Develop a 'Socratic attitude': become aware of what you think and how you think; examine your beliefs; turn your judgments into curiosity.*
- *Embrace wonder: stay away from criticism and defence; move towards a sense of wonder about what makes something happen or be said.*
- *Choose courage and vulnerability over convenience and armour: dare to ask confrontational questions.*
- *Distinguish between judging and condemning: judge, but do so objectively; examine your own judgment and also the opposite of your judgment.*
- *Focus on the other person: try to understand what the other person thinks and feels; avoid your own perspective in this process.*
- *Slow down: think and speak more slowly; practice pausing for twenty seconds before answering a question; reflect on others' words and observe your thoughts.*
- *Don't forget your smile: become wiser together and enjoy the conversations.*

Asking questions is the beginning of wisdom.

A FOURTH HABIT: CONVEYING HOPE AND OPTIMISM

We conclude this book with hope and optimism. We provide a self-test on being hopeful; we explain what being hopeful concretely means and discuss the importance of energy. We introduce an exercise to help you learn to view events more optimistically. Before we delve into hope, we suggest you take the 'hope test'. This can be done very easily through twelve questions, giving you your 'hope score'.

Hope: a 'Tabloid' Test (?)
Rate yourself on the following twelve questions using the scale below:

1 & 2 – Not at all true
3 & 4 – Somewhat untrue
5 & 6 – Somewhat true
7 & 8 – Completely true

1. ____ *I can think of many ways to get out of a jam.*
2. ____ *I energetically pursue my goals.*
3. ____ *I feel tired most of the time.*
4. ____ *There are lots of ways around any problem.*
5. ____ *I am easily downed in an argument.*
6. ____ *I can think of many ways to get the things in life that are important to me.*
7. ____ *I worry about my health.*
8. ____ *Even when others get discouraged, I know I can find a way to solve the problem.*
9. ____ *My past experiences have prepared me well for my future.*
10. ____ *I've been pretty successful in life.*
11. ____ *I usually find myself worrying about something.*
12. ____ *I meet the goals that I set for myself.*

What you have just completed is not a 'Tabloid' test ⌣. You have taken the cognitive 'Adult Hope Scale Test' by American psychologist Snyder (2002). Snyder specialises in the field of positive psychology. He conducted research into human responses to personal feedback, the human need for uniqueness, and hope.

Knowing What We Want, Generating Options, Starting and Persevering

Interest in hope within psychology was initially focused on reducing despair. In positive psychology, hope is about achieving a destination, a goal. Hope is a positive emotion, based on the idea that you are successfully taking steps towards your goal. Hope is the ability to follow a path that leads to a goal. It also helps to stay motivated on that path and to adjust when needed towards the goal. Hope starts from a thought process: 'What is happening and where do we want to go? What qualities can we use to achieve our goal? What in the current context can help us achieve our goals? How did we handle similar situations in the past?'

When we are hopeful:
- We have the willpower to set a goal (goal setting).
- We can map out workable routes to the goal (pathway thinking).
- We find energy and motivation to follow those routes (agency thinking).
- We can come up with and follow new routes in the face of setbacks (agency thinking).

'Pathway Thinking' and 'Agency Thinking'

Much of what we consciously and unconsciously do at work stems from goals. These give us the power to direct our behaviour. Often, they are mapped out in tables and systems. We set targets. We strive to achieve a certain turnover or margin and translate these into 'key performance indicators' (KPIs). We respect 'service level agreements' (SLAs). To be able to 'deliver' on time, we provide 'interim milestones'. Naturally, we also have 'deadlines'. In most professional environments, there is certainly no shortage of objectives. However, to be hopeful, we need more than just objectives. It remains a surprise to us that the lion's share of the attention is directed there. Being hopeful is always a combination of 'willpower' (the will to achieve the goal, or 'agency thinking') and 'waypower' (the route to that goal, or 'pathway thinking'). How do we, together with our employees, give sufficient attention to 'waypower', the movement towards the goal and the energy to keep the engine running? A question well worth exploring further, as evidenced by the case below.

Edward is the HSE Manager (Health, Safety & Environment) for a large construction company. During his annual review meeting, several safety objectives were established. One such objective is that the KPI 'safety gear', which tracks incidents of not wearing safety equipment, must decrease by at least 25%. Additionally, it is expected that a monthly meeting with coworkers regarding extra safety measures will be scheduled at each site. The goal is clear. Edward wants to discuss the pressure he feels from the 'safety gear' KPI. He works towards his objectives with the utmost care and attention, and all meetings are scheduled (pathway thinking). However, the numbers are not decreasing sufficiently. This causes Edward to lose his motivation.

It fills him with fear. When we discuss this, we delve into Edward's approach during these safety meetings at the various sites (agency thinking). Edward feels uncomfortable repeatedly insisting on the mandatory wearing of helmets. He feels like a schoolteacher. We work on changing this belief that is holding Edward back. We look for examples that con-

tradict his belief, situations where he did not feel like a schoolteacher but received understanding for his request. He anchors this positive shift. It energises him. He believes he can adopt this mindset. He leaves with the hopeful conviction that he can achieve the 25% reduction (agency thinking).

Energy and Motivation on the Journey

We often focus strongly on the result and less on the process. The goal occupies us so much that we forget to enjoy the journey towards it. Dao, better known in the West as Tao, means 'Way' or 'Path'. It is a key concept in Taoism, which derives its name from it. According to Taoism, the wealth lies on your path. Along the path of the journey, we grow more than if we were to reach the goal immediately. Here, we can draw a parallel with 'pathway thinking', mapping out feasible routes to the goal. Years of working with coachees in numerous organisations show us that there is still too much focus on the goals, but not on the various options to achieve them. This presents a significant opportunity for us to bring to organisations. When we give more attention and space to our coworkers in discovering the different routes and options towards their objectives, we naturally adopt a coaching attitude. This way, we put our coworkers at the helm of their growth process.

Determining the different routes to achieve objectives deserves more attention. The same goes for discussing the energy and motivation needed to achieve those objectives. Motivation is now a much-discussed and common topic in many organisations in general. However, this topic often remains at a macro level. We gauge the general motivation of employees. We see it as a call for everyone who works with people to delve deeper. How about the 'micro-energy' and 'micro-motivation' of the employees, the motivation for their various objectives? Do we pay enough attention to and have sufficient insight into this? Do we go beyond checking general motivation and examine what exactly in their tasks provides that motivation and energy?

It is not the responsibility of organisations to make everyone happy.

However, it is the responsibility of organisations to outline a framework for hopeful thinking, feeling, and acting, in order to achieve objectives.

In the autumn of 1994, animation studio Pixar was in deep trouble. The company was in the red. The release of Toy Story was scheduled. That film production had significantly exceeded its planned budget. Microsoft had shown interest in buying the company, which would give it access to new 3D graphic design software. This deal also fell through. Pixar's prospects were shaky, but this did not deter the creative team. Despite the financial uncertainty, the team remained optimistic about the future. As they were putting the finishing touches on Toy Story, the filmmakers gathered to brainstorm new projects. The three ideas they came up with? A Bug's Life; Monsters, Inc.; and WALL-E. Each one a blockbuster.

Hope is the Engine, Optimism the Direction

What the team at Pixar did demonstrates optimism. We often see optimism as a personality trait. Think of expressions like: 'That is a true optimist' or 'They see life through rose-tinted glasses'. But what exactly is optimism in positive psychology? Optimism has much in common with hope. Both involve a positive outlook on the future. Both assume that good things will happen. However, they are different. Optimism is a positive attitude about a future event that is likely to happen. Being hopeful is considered more realistic. A hopeful person acknowledges that life may not go as planned but maintains a positive expectation and believes there are various routes to the goal.

Optimism is a feeling of confidence in the future and belief in a positive outcome. On the other hand, there is pessimism: a feeling of doubt, negatively anticipating what is to come. Optimism has many benefits: more positive feelings, stronger relationships with the environment, less anxiety; better acceptance of problems; more perseverance; higher productivity in the workplace.

Optimism and Pessimism: Through Which Lens Do You View The World?
Is it possible to turn a pessimist into an optimist? Optimism is partly in your genes. For some people, it comes very naturally. Additionally, we can enhance optimism through certain techniques. Martin Seligman (Seligman, 1991) researched why people are optimistic and how we can learn to think more optimistically. His Learned Optimism is one of the most widely used interventions to consciously learn to think positively and consequently approach life with a positive mindset. 'Learned optimism' is about managing your own way of 'explaining' situations. We examine what happens when negative and positive events cross our paths. In doing so, three aspects are scrutinised: self, time, and context.

A negative event: not being accepted for a job.

SELF
- The optimist doesn't blame themselves: 'The interview questions were quite tough.'
- The pessimist blames themselves: 'It's my fault. I should have prepared better for the interview.'

TIME
- The optimist sees this as a one-off event: 'It's okay, the next job interview will go better.'
- The pessimist believes this will happen again in the future: 'At the next interview, it will undoubtedly go wrong again.'

CONTEXT

- The optimist isolates the negative event: 'I have many talents. Perhaps the other candidate just had a few more advantages.'
- The pessimist magnifies the negative event: 'This is where I stop dreaming. I'll never find the job of my life.'

And now the opposite, a positive event: being hired for a job

SELF

- The optimist believes they deserve it: 'I did well. I can be proud of myself.'
- The pessimist sees it as pure luck, nothing to do with them: 'Unbelievable, there must have been few good candidates.'

TIME

- The optimist believes this is a sign of more good things to come: 'I have skills and talents that I can rely on in the future as well.'
- The pessimist is convinced the event is a fluke: 'Everyone gets lucky sometimes.'

CONTEXT

- The optimist enlarges the positive event: 'This is a great start to a new phase in my life.'
- The pessimist isolates the positive event: 'I got hired. That doesn't mean I'll succeed in what's expected of me.'

Learning to challenge your thoughts and beliefs and to consider alternative explanations is, according to Seligman, the key to greater optimism. We can investigate concrete evidence for the truth of our beliefs ourselves. Becoming skilled in arguing with ourselves is central to this process. Realising that we can choose how we think about a situation means we can create new thinking patterns: strengthening positive patterns and questioning and changing negative ones.

It is, of course, not a black-and-white story. And yet, believing that we have a favourable influence and can make a positive difference is empowering. Letting go of setbacks and not seeing ourselves too often as the villain of the story allows us to tackle challenges more actively. Optimism is believing that you have influence and can use it to increase your chances of a positive outcome.

Hope and optimism are a choice. We can learn it. It is the engine of success. Hopeful and optimistic people achieve better results and experience higher well-being. They are more grateful and live more harmoniously. They grow old healthier. Moreover, they live longer. In a study conducted in the United States, 97,253 women aged between 50 and 79 were followed for eight years. The risk of death was found to be 14% lower in the group of women who were the most optimistic, compared to those who were at the bottom of the optimism scale.

How we think translates into how we communicate with each other. In positive communication, we convey hope and optimism. We consciously choose to focus on goals, as well as the journey towards them, along with the energy and motivation that come with it. We amplify what is good and challenge 'pessimistic' statements. Positive communication leaves a positive impression on the listener. It promotes well-being for both the speaker and the listener. Making a conscious effort in this regard is a task for every reader of this book.

 A library of questionnaires on hope and optimism can be found on the University of Pennsylvania's website: Meaning in Life; Satisfaction with Life; Well-being; Work-Life; Stress and Empathy. Martin Seligman is the director and a professor of positive psychology at the institution.

Positive communication is not the absence of negative verbal and non-verbal communication. It is the presence of positive, reinforcing, and facilitating conversations and gestures. Positive communication is unique: it has the ability to generate physical, social, and psychological health and well-being. It is communication that promotes happiness, health, and well-being (Socha, 2013). From this shared belief, we explored storytelling, the conscious choice of positive language, the deliberate creation of a forum for interaction, and also hope and optimism, as these are inherent in positive communication.

BACK TO OUR DESIRE

"It is our desire that you, a professional in your field, become convinced of the impact of positive psychology on yourself and others. Together, we ensure well-being, for and with everyone in every organisation with corporate positivity." That's how we started this book.

What do you need to contribute, to become a corporate positivity activist? What are your commitments after reading Team Smile? How do you consciously build a workplace where everyone feels good? We hope you are hungry, that you feel eager to learn, that you dare to struggle. Team and organisational culture belong to everyone, including you.

How do you experience involvement, ambiance, connection, mindset, and communication? And what about your team and your organisation? With the 360° corporate positivity®-scan and the e-learning platform, you will discover everyone's potential to flourish; psychologically, emotionally, and socially, both when things are easy and when they are tough.

For more information on integrating corporate positivity into a team or organisation, please contact: hello@marbl.be or meet our corporate positivity-activist community on www.corporatepositivity.com